Germany
1918-1945

J A Cloake

OXFORD UNIVERSITY PRESS

OXFORD
UNIVERSITY PRESS

Great Clarendon Street, Oxford OX2 6DP

Oxford University Press is a department
of the University of Oxford.

It furthers the University's objective of excellence
in research, scholarship, and education by publishing
worldwide in

Oxford New York

*Athens Auckland Bangkok Bogotá
Buenos Aires Cape Town Chennai
Dar es Salaam Delhi Florence Hong Kong
Istanbul Karachi Kolkata Kuala Lumpur
Madrid Melbourne Mexico City Mumbai
Nairobi Paris São Paulo Shanghai Singapore Taipei
Tokyo Toronto Warsaw*

with associated companies in *Berlin Ibadan*

ISBN 0 19 913277 1

Printed in Spain by Gráficas Estella, S.A.

Publisher's Acknowledgements

The publishers would like to thank the following for
permission to reproduce photographs:
AKG London: pp.12 (top left & bottom right), 14, 21, 22
(top), 24 left, 26 (bottom right), 29, 30, 32, 34 (left), 35
(bottom), 43 (bottom), 49, 55, 59 (top right), 60 (top
right), 74, 78 (both), 80, 90; Archiv Gerstenberg: p. 56;
Associated Press: p. 59 (bottom); Bildarchiv Preussischer
Kulturbesitz: p. 81 (right), 86 (top); Bilderdienst
Suddeutscher Verlag: pp. 4, 6 (top), 9 (top), 10, 12
(bottom left & middle)), 17, 19 (right), 24 (right), 25
(right), 27, 35 (top), 36, 40 (left), 42 (top left), 45
(both), 46, 47 (top), 57, 60 (bottom), 63, 64, 66
(inset), 71 (left), 73 (middle), 76 (top), 83 (bottom), 86
(bottom), 87 (left), 91 (both), 93; British Film Institute:
pp. 58 (bottom), 59 (top left); British Library/Sunday
Despatch: p. 94 (bottom); British Library/The Nation: p.
95; British Library Newspaper Library/Daily Express
(4.3.33): p. 40 (right); British Library Newspaper
Library/Vorwarts: p.20 (top); British Library Newspaper
Library/Washington Post (16.2.24): p. 19 (left);
Bundesarchiv Koblenz: Cover, pp: 20 (bottom), 81 (left),
83 (top); Camera Press: p. 69 (top left); The Centre for the
Study of Cartoons and Caricature/Daily Herald (3.7.34): p.
47 (bottom); E.T. Archive: p. 75; Hulton Getty Picture
Collection Ltd: pp. 13 (bottom right), 48, 58 (top), 67, 72,
73 (bottom), 94 (top left); Imperial War Museum: pp. 12
(middle left), 13 bottom left & middle & middle right), 18,
26 (top right), 28, 62 (left), 82; Institute of Contempory
History and Wiener Library Ltd: pp. 54, 66 (main), 77,
79, 84; Ella Liebermann-Shiber: pp. 68 (bottom left), 69
(top right); Ella Liebermann-Shiber/Panstwowe Muzeum
Oswiecim Brzezinka: p.69 (bottom); The Marquess of Bath,
Longleat House, Warminster, Wiltshire: p. 70; National
Museum of American Art, Smithsonian Institution, Peter A
Juley & Son Collection: p 57; Punch: p. 26 (top left); Punch
(19.2.19): p 13 (top); Punch (15.8.23): p 16; Punch
(8.3.33): p. 42 (right); Stadtarchiv Northeim
Fotosammlung: p. 50; Ullstein Bilderdienst: pp. 31 (top &
middle), 61, 68 (top & middle), 73 (top left); Weimar
Archive: pp.9 (bottom), 15, 25 (left), 52, 53, 60 (top
left), 87 (right); Weimar Archive/Simplicissimus: p.6
(middle & bottom), 22 (bottom), 31 (bottom),34 (right);
Weidenfeld Archive: pp. 71 (right); Dr George Wittenstein:
p. 89.

The publishers have made every effort to trace the
copyright holders of all photographs, but in some cases
have been unable to do so. They would welcome any
information which would enable them to rectify this.

Designed by Peter Tucker, Holbrook Design Oxford Ltd.

All illustrations are by Peter Tucker

Contents

Preface

Germany 1918–1945 has a detailed and comprehensive text that is accessible to the majority of GCSE students. Each chapter of the book has a clear and sharp focus. Attention has been given to the amount of time likely to be allotted to a study of this kind within a GCSE course.

The book is designed to be used flexibly. As aspects of the rise of the Nazis and Weimar politics can be difficult to grasp, teachers and students may wish firstly to consider the question, 'What was life like in Germany after 1933?' or 'How did life in Germany change under the Nazis?'. Secondly the question of how such a regime came to power can be tackled.

Each chapter commences with a quotation that summarises or illuminates the history to be studied. Teachers may choose to use it as starting point for enquiry or return to it and seek a contextual explanation after study. Each chapter easily lends itself to timeline exercises that establish a chronology of important events.

The design of *Germany 1918–1945* recognises the wealth of material that already exists on this topic. For this reason the Versailles Treaty is summarised on pages 12–13 and combined with images of events that stimulate a broader understanding. Teachers will be able to use the book easily in their teaching and incorporate their existing resources.

Many of the extracts from other historical works are deliberately substantial to allow for the proper treatment of interpretations. Line numbering has been included for these sources to assist in their detailed study and class discussion.

Research exercises utilise existing resources, develop knowledge and help ensure a clear theme is followed in each chapter.

Throughout the book key questions have been answered directly in separate sections. These key questions are either specified in the GCSE syllabuses or are those most frequently asked by students. By using these key question sections the teacher will have a definite starting point for further analysis.

To study the history of Germany between 1918 and 1945, is surely to learn lessons that are essential for the citizen of a modern democracy.

1 *Germany before Weimar*

> I have asked His Majesty to bring into government those who are responsible for the state we are in. They must now make the peace that has to be made. They are going to have to eat the soup they have cooked for us!

General Ludendorff explains the situation to his officers on 1 October 1918. A comment often seen as the beginnings of the 'stab-in-the-back' myth.

Kaiser Wilhelm II (centre) discussing the progress of the war with Field Marshal Hindenburg (left) and General Ludendorff in 1917

Before 1918 Germany was ruled by the Kaiser or Emperor. He appointed his Chancellor and ministers as the Government. They, in turn, made decisions and wrote laws which were approved by the Reichstag. This system of government was supported by important groups of people in Germany such as army officers, civil servants, judges, university teachers, landowners, and businessmen. These groups were socially connected, e.g. between 1898 and 1918, 56% of army officers had a noble title. For a long time these groups were the main sources of power in German life and politics.

Germany's system of government had served her well. In the late nineteenth century Germany was very prosperous. Its industrial and military power grew. The German middle classes were happy with the system of government which provided so much security, jobs, and prosperity. They had no reason to want more democracy or political power for themselves. Indeed many middle class people were more worried about the growing German trade unions with their Socialist ideas.

German trade unions had grown to a massive 2.5 million members by 1913. Their full time leaders were moderates who wanted to work with the Government. The unions supported their own political party, the Social Democrats (SPD). The spectacular rise of the SPD to be the biggest party in the Reichstag was the major event of pre-war German politics. The majority of the SPD, like the unions, were moderates. They were committed to working peacefully to improve the conditions of German workers. The party had a more extreme section whose most able speaker was Rosa Luxemburg. She proposed a more revolutionary role for trade unions in Germany and believed in the Communist ideas.

Relations between the Government and the unions became difficult in the pre-war years. In a number of key industries, as wages and living standards declined, there followed strikes that embittered the Government and businessmen. In 1912 the SPD won 36% of the votes for the Reichstag and it became difficult for the Government to obtain agreement for its budget. Thus, early in 1914, the outlook in Germany was gloomy. On 28 June 1914 the assassination of the Austrian Crown Prince Franz Ferdinand offered the Kaiser Wilhelm and his government a way to escape their problems.

When the First World War broke out, the German Chancellor, Bethmann-Hollweg, cleverly blamed Russia, and because of this, he obtained support for the war from the majority of the SPD in the Reichstag. A minority in the SPD opposed the war. They said that the war was not to defend Germany but to expand it. One representative, Karl Liebknecht, courageously even voted against the money to finance the war. As the war progressed, the split between the two groups of the SPD became wider. In 1915 critics of the war in the SPD were thrown out of the Party and they later formed an Independent Socialist Party (USP) under Hugo Haase. For the remaining years of the war, the SPD officials and trade union leaders worked hard to maintain a united front and counter mounting criticism of the war amongst the workers. The USP, on the other hand, opposed the war. They wanted to end it and then to change the system that had brought it about in the first place.

As the war continued and the allied blockade of ports hit home, ordinary Germans suffered more and more. There were shortages of food, medicines and clothing. Early in 1918 Germany's generals began to realise that they would lose the war. They advised the Kaiser to ask for peace. He knew the situation was desperate. Germany seemed close to revolution at home. If Germany became more democratic she might gain a better peace settlement from the allies. And there was the need to shift the blame for the war away from himself and the army, the traditional sources of power, to suitable scapegoats. In October 1918 the Kaiser acted. He chose members of the SPD dominated Reichstag to form a new government to negotiate a peace.

But the changes came too late to halt the unrest and dissatisfaction with the war. Early in November 1918, the system of government was criticised and threatened. Mass meetings were held against the war. The German navy mutinied in Kiel on

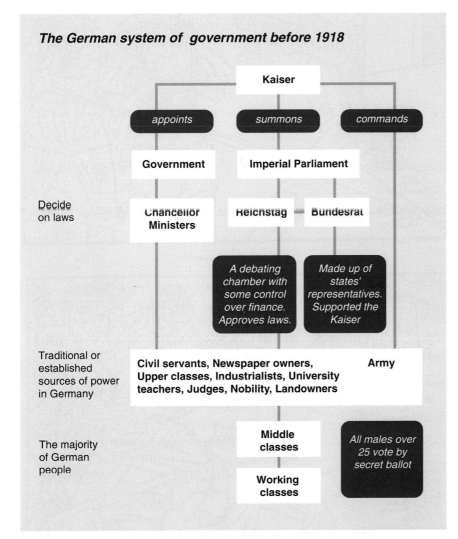

The German system of government before 1918

Kaiser

appoints — summons — commands

Government — Imperial Parliament

Decide on laws

Chancellor Ministers — Reichstag — Bundesrat

A debating chamber with some control over finance. Approves laws.

Made up of states' representatives. Supported the Kaiser

Traditional or established sources of power in Germany

Civil servants, Newspaper owners, Upper classes, Industrialists, University teachers, Judges, Nobility, Landowners — Army

The majority of German people

Middle classes

All males over 25 vote by secret ballot

Working classes

Phillip Scheidemann proclaims the new
Republic on 9 November 1918

3 November at the prospect of orders for a
suicide attack on the British navy so close
to the end of the war. Groups of workers
and soldiers joined in and took over key
towns and cities. Revolution was in the air.
It reminded many people of what
happened in Russia in 1917. By 9
November the capital, Berlin, had been
taken over. The army generals told Kaiser
Wilhelm that he had to give up the throne
to save Germany from civil war. Without
the support of the army the Kaiser
abdicated. The SPD took advantage of the
great enthusiasm for change. The old split
between the SPD and the USP seemed to
have healed. Both parties supported a new
government with the SPD leader, Friedrich
Ebert, as Chancellor. The SPD made
themselves appear as the leaders of the
revolution, promising that soon the war
would be over, and a fairer, Socialist
Germany would emerge. The old sources
of power would be overthrown. They
quickly swept away the old Imperial
system of government and made Germany
a parliamentary democracy. Censorship
was lifted and the right to union
membership restored. The armistice
agreement to end the war was signed on
11 November 1918.

1   How did the First World War affect
    German politics?

1917: „Schonet eure Feinde!"

1919: „Mordet eure Brüder!"

A cartoon from 1919 unfairly contrasts Karl
Liebknecht's attitudes to the war and the
Spartacist rising (page 9). In 1917 Liebknecht
is saying 'Spare your enemies'. In 1919 he is
saying 'Murder your brothers'. Both Liebknecht
and Luxemburg had argued against the rising
fearing great bloodshed but were outvoted.

AUTOCRACY

LEFT

RIGHT

Communism Socialism Liberalism Conservatism Fascism

KPD USP SPD DDP ZP DVP DNVP NSDAP

The terms *Left* and *Right* to describe political views date back to the French Revolution. At the first meeting of the Estates General (parliament) in 1789, groups of people with the same ideas sat together. Those who supported the king sat on his right and those who opposed him, the Radicals, sat to his left. Those people to the right of the king wanted to keep the old system of government and were opposed to change, whereas those on the left were revolutionaries and wanted change.

Left Wing

- Anti-Fascist
- Opposes Capitalism
- A belief that the workers should have power
- An emphasis on equality
- A stress on social class
- Welcomes change
- Internationalist

Right Wing

- Anti-Communist
- Supports Capitalism
- A belief in the leadership of those who are wise and able
- Acknowledges differences between individuals
- A stress on family and nationality
- Resists changes, prefers traditional ways
- Nationalist

Major German political parties (and date of founding) 1918–1933

KPD **German Communist Party (1918)**
Attracted new members from the young and unemployed in the 1930s. Fought the Nazis in the streets. Strong links with Russian Communists. Dissolved 1933 and some 8,000 members fled abroad.

USP **Independent Socialists Party (1917)**
SPD splinter group. The majority joined the KPD in 1920, the rest returned to the SPD in 1922.

SPD **Social Democratic Party (1875)**
Largest party in the Reichstag in 1914. Supported by workers and lower middle class. Lost support to the KPD in the Depression. Strong supporter of the Weimar Republic. Banned in 1933.

DDP **German Democratic Party (1918)**
Left wing Liberal Party backed by business. Helped draft the Weimar Constitution but lost support when the DVP was formed.

DVP **German People's Party (1918)**
Right wing Liberal party started by Stresemann. Initially opposed to Weimar. It took part in governments and represented the interests of the upper middle class and employers. Lost support in the Depression to smaller parties and the Nazis.

DNVP **German National People's Party (1918)**
Right wing nationalist party. Rejected the Weimar system and Versailles. Strong defender of large landowning interests. Some support from urban middle class and co-operated with the Nazis during the last years of Weimar

NSDAP **National Socialist German Workers' Party (1919)**
Renamed in 1920, relaunched in 1925 and spread beyond Bavaria. Its ideas, policies and supporters came from the right, nationalist and conservative groups. Using propaganda and violence it created a mass electoral following.

ZP **Centre Party (1870)**
Formed to defend Catholic interests. Supported Weimar and took votes from Catholic workers and lower middle class. Centre Party moved to the right in the Depression.

2 *T*he birth of the Weimar Republic

> We are perhaps lost if we do not sign the Treaty, but we are certainly lost if we do sign it.

Gustav Stresemann writing about the Versailles Treaty, 14 May 1919.

The SPD arranged for a general election and a new National Assembly whose first job would be to draw up a new constitution. Although appearing to lead the revolution, the SPD were worried about its direction. They feared that the power they had gained in October might be hijacked by revolutionary left wing groups during the unrest of November 1918. So the SPD leader, Friedrich Ebert, made secret agreements with the new head of the German military, General Groener, to respect the authority of the army officers in return for his support. Shortly afterwards, a deal was struck by the trade union leader, Karl Legien, with Hugo Stinnes, representing German industrialists, to respect private ownership and a free market in return for an 8 hour working day and the recognition of trade unions. These agreements between the traditional sources of power like the army and big business were a way for them to keep influence and prevent more radical change. For the SPD they ensured a peaceful move into power and strengthened their hand against the more extreme left wing parties.

Naturally the USP were disappointed with the way the changes were going. They were more radical; for them the old sources of power, especially the army, had to be reformed if not replaced. But a revolution on the Russian lines, they believed, was not appropriate for Germany. More extreme still were the supporters of Rosa Luxemburg and Karl Liebknecht, from the Spartacus League. They started a new party, the German Communist party (KPD), which criticised the other Socialists, calling them 'Social Fascists' for betraying the workers. They wanted to take the revolution a stage further and make Germany a Communist state like Russia. KPD plans alarmed the German middle classes. They knew how Russian Communists shared out privately owned land, took over banks and factories, and terrorised or killed their opponents.

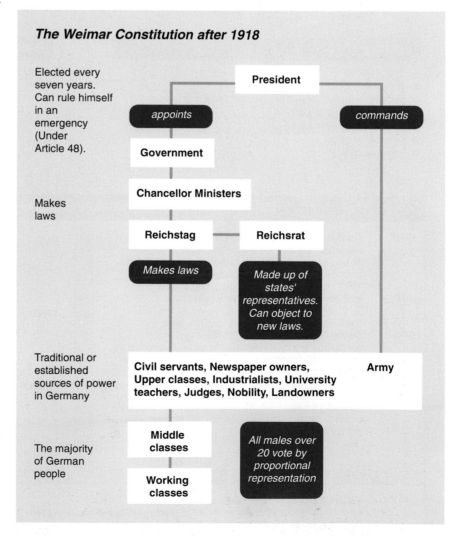

The Weimar Constitution after 1918

Elected every seven years. Can rule himself in an emergency (Under Article 48). → **President** — *appoints* / *commands*

appoints → **Government** → **Chancellor Ministers**

Makes laws → **Reichstag** / **Reichsrat**

Makes laws (Reichstag)

Made up of states' representatives. Can object to new laws. (Reichsrat)

Traditional or established sources of power in Germany: **Civil servants, Newspaper owners, Upper classes, Industrialists, University teachers, Judges, Nobility, Landowners** **Army**

The majority of German people: **Middle classes**, **Working classes**

All males over 20 vote by proportional representation

Spartacists defend their positions made of rolls of newsprint against attacks from the *Freikorps* in January 1919

These political differences about Germany's future could not be contained for long. Fighting broke out in December 1918 and peaked in January 1919. The USP withdrew from the government leaving the SPD in charge. Spartacist supporters had to act quickly before the election. On 5 January they tried to take over the government in a *Putsch* in Berlin which succeeded in gaining control of some newspaper offices. Their rebellion was ruthlessly crushed by the *Freikorps*. Set up by Ebert, these new military units were made up of former soldiers who had no sympathy with the workers. They were directed to this work by Gustav Noske, the SPD Defence Minister, who relished the task of destroying the opposition of militant left-wing workers. Luxemburg and Liebknecht were brutally murdered. By 13 January the Spartacist Putsch had failed. On 19 January 1919 the general elections to the new National Parliament were held.

'Cheers Noske – The workers are disarmed', says the *Freikorps* officer in this cartoon by George Grosz. What does this tell us about the *Freikorps* and the cartoonist's view of them?

Left wing supporters of Karl Liebknecht and Rosa Luxemburg protest in February 1919 at their assassinations

liberal party) and the Zentrum Party received more than three quarters of the vote. The right wing and conservative parties did poorly in the election. However, the election did not end left wing threats to the Government. Groups of workers disillusioned with the lack of progress towards further democracy staged uprisings in the industrial centres of Germany. Indeed an uprising in Berlin so worried the new members of the Parliament that they preferred to hold their first meetings in the safer and quieter town of Weimar, from which the new state took its name, rather than the capital. The *Freikorps* continued their bloody work of putting down these workers' rebellions which were never properly led or organised enough to succeed.

1   What motivated the following groups of people?
    a The leaders of the SPD
    b Supporters of left-wing groups like the Spartacists
    c The army and industrialists

The results of the election seemed a victory for peaceful democratic parliamentary government. The 'Weimar' parties – the SPD, the DDP (a progressive

What effect did the November 1918 revolution and the Spartacist Putsch have upon the politics of Weimar Germany?

The result of this period was important for the new government. It was forced into closer co-operation with the traditional sources of power in Germany. These more conservative forces in Germany, the judges, the civil servants, the army, industrialists, and the newspapers owners were in turn able to reclaim some of their influence on the direction the country was taking. In the election the SPD made good use of the idea of the Communist threat. It was obvious to the other left-wing parties, the USP and KPD, that there was little prospect of further democratic change. The SPD lost the support of many German workers who believed that the new

Republic had sold out. They now backed the newer left-wing parties. The power of the Left and the labour movement was divided amongst itself. The USP and KPD wanted important industries like coal and steel taken over by the State. Here the workers were most militant and the industrialists most powerful. However little change could be made without alienating important supporters of the SPD government. Thus an opportunity was missed that might have removed the workers' taste for revolution and led to a more democratic system of government in Germany.

The most difficult problem for the new Weimar government was the Treaty which ended the First World War. It was signed at Versailles on 28 June 1919. The victorious powers, Britain, France and America met in Paris to discuss the terms of the peace. The Treaty contained 440 clauses; they covered responsibility for causing the war as well as financial compensation for the damage suffered. Other important clauses removed large areas of land from Germany and reduced her armed forces significantly. The final terms of the Treaty provoked a storm of protest in Germany. Some members of the new Weimar Republic's government resigned including the new Chancellor, Phillip Scheidemann who had taken over

after Ebert became the first President. A new government was formed and, after heated debate, the Reichstag accepted the Treaty on 28 June 1919.

Research

2 What attitudes did the leaders of Britain, France and America have towards the peace settlement with Germany?
3 What were Woodrow Wilson's 14 Points?
4 What were some of the precise terms of the Versailles Treaty, 1919?
5 Why did Germans object so strongly to the Versailles Treaty?

Election results of major parties (**percentage of vote** and *seats won*) in German General Elections during the Weimar Republic 1919–1933 (see also page 38)

Party	1919 January	1920 June	1924 May	1924 December	1928 May	1930 September	1932 July	1932 November	1933 March
National Socialists NSDAP	–	–	6.6	3.0	2.6	18.3	37.3	33.1	43.9
Seats	–	–	32	14	12	107	230	196	288
Conservatives DNVP	10.3	14.9	19.5	20.5	14.2	7.0	5.9	8.8	8.0
Seats	44	71	95	103	73	41	37	52	52
National Liberals DVP	4.4	13.9	9.2	10.1	8.7	4.5	1.2	1.9	1.1
Seats	19	65	45	51	45	30	7	11	2
Centre Zentrum	19.7	17.9	16.6	17.3	15.1	14.8	15.9	15.0	14.1
Seats	111	80	84	85	81	90	95	88	74
Liberal Progressives DDP	18.6	8.3	5.7	6.3	4.9	3.8	1.0	1.0	0.9
Seats	75	39	28	32	25	20	4	2	5
Social Democrats SPD	37.9	21.6	20.5	26.0	29.8	24.5	21.6	20.4	18.2
Seats	163	102	100	131	153	143	133	121	120
Independent Socialists USP	7.6	17.9	0.8	0.3	0.1	–	–	–	–
Seats	22	84	–	–	–	–	–	–	–
Communists KPD		2.1	12.6	9.0	10.6	13.1	14.3	16.9	12.2
Seats		4	62	45	54	77	89	100	81
Others	1.5	3.4	8.5	7.4	14.0	14.0	2.8	2.9	1.6
Seats	7	10	29	29	51	72	11	12	7

Adolf Hitler and the Treaty of Versailles 1919 – 1939

Northern Schleswig and Holstein to Denmark

Eupen & Malmedy to Belgium

German army banned from 50 km of Rhineland

Allies occupy Rhineland

Use of Saar coal for France

Alsace & Lorraine to France

Map showing: DENMARK, GREAT BRITAIN, NETHERLANDS, GERMANY, BELGIUM, Saar (Plebiscite in 1935), FRANCE, SWITZERLAND, ITALY. Scale 0 — 400 km. N (north arrow)

- German army reduced to 100,000 men
- No tanks
- No submarines
- No warplanes

What a use could be made of the Treaty of Versailles. How each of its points could be branded in the hearts and minds of the German people until they find their souls aflame with rage and shame and a will of steel is forged with the common cry, "We will have arms again !".

Adolf Hitler, *Mein Kampf*, 1925

1 A 1924 DNVP election poster accusing the SPD of betraying the German army in 1918
2 German troops re-enter the demilitarised Rhineland in 1936
3 Tanks at a Nazi parade, 1936
4 A cartoon from an American newspaper, 18 October 1936. At this time there was a great interest outside Germany in the growing support for the Nazis.
5 *Stuka* dive bombers being armed for the *Blitzkrieg* on Poland, September 1939. German forces like these gained valuable experience fighting in the Spanish Civil War from July 1936.

Memel
to Lithuania

Danzig
controlled by
League
of Nations

Posen
& West Prussia to
form a 'Polish corridor'
given to Poland

Hultschin
to Czechoslovakia

Eastern
Upper Silesia
to Poland

Treaty
of St. Germain, 1919
took Bohemia & Moravia
from Austria for the new
state of Czechoslovakia

Germany
forbidden to join
with Austria

GIVING HIM ROPE?

German Criminal (to Allied Police). "HERE, I SAY, STOP! YOU'RE HURTING ME! [Aside.]
IF I ONLY WHINE ENOUGH I MAY BE ABLE TO WRIGGLE OUT OF THIS YET."

- Germany guilty of causing war – War Guilt Clause
- Germany to pay compensation – Reparations
- Over 70,000 sq. km. of Germany given to other countries, which was 13% of her territory and 10% of her former population
- All German colonies taken away

> My programme was to abolish the Treaty of Versailles. It is nonsense to pretend I didn't reveal this until 1933 or 1935 or 1937. I have written and rewritten a thousand times these words – The abolition of the Treaty of Versailles.

Adolf Hitler in a speech made in Berlin on 20 January 1941.

6 German troops entering Austria in March 1938.
7 Adolf Hitler receives the acclaim of the Reichstag after the *Anschluss* or union with Austria in March 1938.
8 Sudetenland Germans greet Hitler in October 1938.
9 Czech citizens react to the German army entering Prague on 15 March 1939.
10 A cartoon from *Punch*, 19 February 1919, reveals a British attitude to Germany.

3 *T*he challenge of the Right

> You may pronounce us guilty a thousand times but history will smile and tear to tatters the sentence of this court.

Hitler's final speech at his trial, 1924.

The Weimar Republic overcame the first challenge to its authority from the Spartacists and militant workers in 1919 by using the paramilitary *Freikorps*. In 1920 some of those very *Freikorps* troops turned on the Weimar Government and tried to overthrow it. They were angered by the Government's order to disband army units to agree with the terms of the Versailles Treaty. *Freikorps* units near Berlin decided to act to prevent this. They seized the capital and set up a new government under the control of Wolfgang Kapp, an extreme right-wing politician. The Weimar Government asked the head of the German army, General Hans von Seekt, to help crush the revolt. He refused, announcing that 'the German army does not shoot upon the German army'. The anxious Government fled to Stuttgart in south-west Germany where they felt safer.

However, the Kapp Putsch, as it became known, disintegrated very quickly because of the actions of the German workers. The Government called a general strike which paralysed all communications and the country came to a standstill. Many senior army, police officers and civil servants sympathised with Kapp but realising that the revolt was failing, did not join in. Within four days the revolt was over and the Weimar Government returned to Berlin. Despite the fact that about 500 people were directly involved with the Kapp Putsch only about 100 were charged, even fewer were sentenced. Some of the workers

who staged the general strike, especially in the Ruhr coal mines and steel works, carried on with it. Having shown their power they hoped to pressurise the Government into more social and economic change. This time, when requested, the army did lend a hand with the *Freikorps* to restore order. The workers' armed revolt was put down with much bloodshed and hundreds killed.

Zu den Unruhen in Berlin.
Ein Panzerzug inmitten der Stadt.

 Freikorps troops arrive in Berlin aboard an armoured train in March 1920

The result of the 1920 election was a severe blow for the SPD. To survive in government it had to form coalitions with the Centre Party and right-wing German People's Party (DVP) which to begin with was anti-Republican. The USP were very successful in the 1920 election. This encouraged the USP leaders to make closer links with the Communists in Moscow, with the result that just under half the membership left the USP to join the more extreme left wing German Communists (KPD). With their new found strength the KPD decided that they would try to overthrow the Government. Their uprising in central Germany in March 1921 was put down, like the Spartacists' Putsch had been, by the German army. This was the last attempt by the left-wing of German politics to take over the Government by violent means. Although the *Freikorps* had been disbanded after helping to suppress the Ruhr revolt, right-wing terrorism continued. Between 1921 and 1923, 356 Socialists and Communists were murdered by right-wing supporters, notably the Centre politician, Mathias Erzberger and the Foreign Minister, Walther Rathenau.

Apart from political challenges to the Weimar Republic, the biggest test for its government followed the announcement of the Versailles reparation terms in April 1921. The Allies calculated the sum at £6,600 million, to be repaid at the rate of £100 million every year as well as 25% of the value of Germany's annual exports. Apart from the colossal size of this amount, Germany had another problem. She had borrowed heavily to pay for fighting the war. So now she owed money on two counts. The German Government could have increased taxation to pay the debts but this would depress the economy, cause unemployment and make matters worse. Instead the Government simply printed more paper money which meant the mark was worth less and inflation started.

The Weimar Government found the money to pay the first instalment of reparations, £50 million in the summer of 1921 but early in 1922 fell behind with their payments and spent the rest of the year arguing with the Allies that the payments were too high. France, who stood to receive much of this money, lost patience and decided that she would go into Germany and take what was owed. In January 1923 French and Belgian troops marched into the industrial heartland of the Ruhr. Anger at the French action swept across Germany. Workers went on strike, and right-wing supporters carried out acts of sabotage. The Weimar Government called for a campaign of 'passive

resistance' and German industry ground to a halt. German inflation accelerated, and the value of the mark compared with the dollar or pound plummeted. It was a time of *hyper inflation*. Middle class Germans who had savings found that they had become poor overnight. Their view of the Weimar Republic reached a new low. Workers on strike had no income and they faced starvation. Those with a wage found it would not buy enough food. Some workers collected their wages in wheelbarrows. The price of a cup of coffee

'No You can't force me !' A German poster encouraging passive resistance to the French occupation of the Ruhr in 1923.

THE EXCHANGE ASYLUM.

ROUBLE. "WHAT'S YOUR NAME?"
MARK. "MARK."
ROUBLE. "WHAT ARE YOU DOING?"
MARK. "FALLING."
ROUBLE. "WHAT'S YOUR FACE VALUE?"
MARK. "A SHILLING."
ROUBLE. "WHAT ARE YOU WORTH NOW?"
MARK. "TWENTY MILLION TO THE POUND."
ROUBLE. "COME INSIDE."
FRANC (nervously). "I'M NOT FEELING TOO SANE MYSELF."

A cartoon from the British magazine *Punch* on 15 April 1923 comments on the 'insane' inflation in Germany at this time

could double in the time it took to drink it. The future of the Weimar Republic hung in the balance in 1923. It was at this point in southern Germany that Adolf Hitler mounted his first challenge to the Weimar Government.

Research
1   How did the value of the German mark change between 1914 and 1923?

The President, Friedrich Ebert, used his powers under Article 48 of the Weimar Constitution to appoint a new government under Gustav Stresemann to end the crisis over the French occupation. Passive resistance to the French in the Ruhr was ended and Germany started paying reparations again. The leader of the Bavarian State Government, Gustav von Kahr, called a meeting on the night of 8 November, 1923, in the Buergerbräu beer hall, to debate the Government's new policies. Adolf Hitler was a minor right-wing politician in southern Germany at this time. His idea was to hijack the meeting, and to persuade the senior politicians, police and army officers present to help him to take over the State Government. Hitler interrupted Kahr after about 20 minutes with a shot that was fired into the ceiling. Hitler announced that his revolution had begun and no one could leave. He took Kahr and his companions into a private room while his brown-shirted storm troopers watched over the excited audience. Once alone Hitler tried to win them over to his idea of setting up a separate government in Bavaria and then marching on Berlin to overthrow the national Weimar Government. He said he had the support of the First World War General, Ludendorff. Hitler also threatened them with a revolver. They agreed to support him. But when Hitler left to announce his success to the beer hall, Kahr and the others slipped away to prepare to crush the Nazis' Putsch (see page 28). When Hitler marched into the state capital, Munich, the next morning with 3,000 storm troopers, he was met by well armed and prepared police. At the centre of the city the police opened fire. The firing lasted for about a minute. Sixteen storm troopers lay dead and many others were wounded. Ludendorff was arrested. Hitler escaped but was captured two days later and charged with treason.

Hitler's punishment was as lenient as that handed out to the leaders of the Kapp Putsch in 1920. Ludendorff was acquitted. Hitler was found guilty of treason. Instead

of the life sentence he might have expected he was sentenced to only 5 years. So moved were the jury by Hitler's passionate speeches in court that they asked the judge to reduce this further. Hitler, in fact, spent 9 months in prison where, comfortably placed in his own cell, he wrote a book, his great political work, *Mein Kampf*, (My Struggle).

2   The authority of the Weimar Government was challenged by the Kapp (1920) and Munich (1923) Putsches.
   a Why did each Putsch start?
   b Why did each Putsch fail?
3   What were the effects of the French Invasion of the Ruhr, 1923?

A painting made in 1933 of Hitler addressing the audience of the Munich Beer Hall during the Putsch of 1923. What impression does it give? Why would the Nazis have produced a picture about a failed Putsch?

Why was the Weimar Republic able to overcome the early challenges of right and left-wing groups?

Neither the left or right–wing groups who threatened the Weimar Republic were strong, organised or united enough to overthrow the Government. They did not offer a clear or attractive enough alternative to Weimar. The right-wing political parties went along with an SPD coalition in government to keep the social peace in Germany so the Republic survived.

The Kapp Putsch shows that the Weimar Republic enjoyed little support from the established sources of power in Germany which favoured the Right. Left-wing workers were always severely dealt with. The Kapp Putsch served as a warning to the army later in 1923 of the danger of rash action.

Gustav Stresemann's talent and resolve stabilised a dangerous situation for the Weimar Republic. Inflation in the 1920s did not cause as much desperation and suffering as mass unemployment in the 1930s.

4   What evidence can you find in this and the previous chapter to support these conclusions?

4 *Weimar Success 1924–1929*

A DDP poster from 1924 reminding voters of the difficulties that Weimar has overcome and the threat of extreme political parties

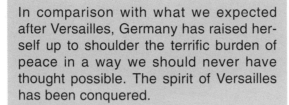

In comparison with what we expected after Versailles, Germany has raised herself up to shoulder the terrific burden of peace in a way we should never have thought possible. The spirit of Versailles has been conquered.

German journalist Victor Schiff, writing in 1929.

Between 1924 and 1929 Germany recovered from some of her earlier problems. The man behind this recovery was Gustav Stresemann who agreed to become Chancellor in September 1923. Stresemann was a right-wing politician who, like others in the DVP and also later the DNVP, realised that they had to play a more constructive role in the political life of the Weimar Republic. The alternative was to let Germany descend into chaos and anarchy. The practical benefits of forming a coalition of centre and right-wing parties was that they would keep the Socialist SPD out of power. It was Stresemann who resumed reparations payments and called off passive resistance to the French in the Ruhr. A new bank was set up which issued a new currency, the Rentenmark, that could be exchanged for the old devalued currency. Stresemann remained as Chancellor until the end of 1923 when he became Foreign Minister.

It was as Foreign Minister that Stresemann did some of his most important work. Weimar Germany needed friends in the West. In April 1922 the then German Foreign Minister, Walther Rathenau, had surprised and alarmed Western countries by signing a trade agreement with the Soviet Union. The Rapallo Agreement, as it was known, allowed for exports and a development of weapons away from Allied supervision. It also angered right-wing Germans that they should be dealing with a Communist state like Russia and they assassinated Rathenau in June 1922. Stresemann had the job of repairing relations with the West.

Stresemann's first success was to negotiate the Dawes Plan in 1924. The Dawes Plan aimed to prevent a crisis over reparations like the one in 1923. It did not reduce what Germany owed but reorganised the repayments more sensibly in staged payments. Over the next five years Germany would make repayments starting at £50 million and rising to £125 million. Afterwards payments would be linked to the prosperity of the German economy. The other part of the Dawes Plan aimed to boost German prosperity by massive injections of American cash. It began by loaning 800 million gold marks to Germany. Dawes started American companies and banks pouring money, nearly $3,000 million by 1930, into Germany. The results were spectacular. German industry produced more goods and exports rose. Unemployment fell and most Germans were better off.

clauses discontinued. Locarno went some way to removing the bitterness that remained after the war. In September 1926 came an even greater success for Stresemann. Germany was given a permanent seat on the Council of the League of Nations. This marked a return to 'Great Power status' for Germany. It was a bold move for Stresemann because many Germans regarded the League as the guardian of the hated Treaty of Versailles. Stresemann intended to show the rest of Europe that Germany had changed and that there was a good case for easing the burdens on her.

Talking Business

▲ A cartoon from *The Washington Post*, 16 February 1924, which shows Allied suspicions of Stresemann's motives in reorganising German reparations

Then Stresemann set about improving Germany's image abroad. In October 1925 Germany signed the Locarno Pact with France, Belgium, Britain, and Italy. By this agreement the countries agreed to keep the existing borders between Germany, France and Belgium. The Ruhr was finally evacuated of foreign troops and the Commission supervising the disarmament

Stresemann's work paid off. His last international success was the Young Plan. Signed in 1930, the plan significantly reduced Germany's reparations from the original £6,600 million to £1,850 million. The length of time Germany had to pay was extended by another 59 years at an average of 2.05 billion marks a year. It allowed for some flexibility in payments if Germany got into difficulty. Before the negotiations had finished, Stresemann, aged 51, died of a heart attack on 8 October 1929.

▲ Gustav Stresemann speaking to the League of Nations Assembly in Geneva. Stresemann was awarded the Nobel Peace Prize on 10 December 1926.

Entgangenes Ziel.

The nurse says, 'You're late Gentlemen, he (Stresemann) is dead.' in this German cartoon from 1929. Right wing Germans like Hugenberg, pursue him with stink bombs and manure and signs calling him a traitor.

„Sie kommen zu spät, meine Herren! — Er ist tot.‟

1 What was Stresemann's greatest achievement?
2 What similarities are there in Sources F and H?
3 What similarities are there in Sources B, C, E and G?

Weimar recovery 1924–1929?

'Rising from the mire'. A DNVP 1924 election poster.

The popular rosy view of Weimar in the 1920s has some truth. German heavy industry, coal and steel, recovered quickly to exceed 1913 production levels in 1928. Exports rose by 40% between 1925 and 1929. Hourly wages rose in every year from 1924 to 1930. There were generous improvements to pensions and sickness benefits schemes and unemployment insurance for 17 million workers was introduced in 1927. Many open signs of consumer prosperity supported the view that Weimar enjoyed boom conditions.

However the rapidity of the German recovery was deceptive. There was economic growth but the balance of trade was consistently in the red. Unemployment never fell below 1.3 million in this period and it was averaging 1.9 million during 1929. The population increased during the 1920s pushing up the jobless total. With grain production only ever three quarters of the 1913 figures, farmers who made one third of the population, faced declining incomes due to the fall in world prices. German savers who lost their money in the post war inflation had little confidence to commit their money again. So money for investment had to be borrowed from abroad. The Germany economy depended on foreign money. Government finances were likewise a cause for concern. The Government balanced the budget in 1924 but from then on had a deficit. Rather than cut back they spent more and borrowed from abroad to pay for it. A German bank's annual report in 1928 referred to 'the complete inner weakness of our economy. We are overloaded with taxes and over high social welfare payments and reparations payments hold back growth.' All this suggests the German economy was in a precarious state long before the Depression. It was in a crisis before a crisis!

But what of the political recovery? The 'Grand Coalition' of SPD, DDP, DVP and Centre parties after the election of 1928 enjoyed the support of over 60% of the Reichstag. That suggests some broad agreements had been reached. In fact it disguises the weakness of the Weimar system. Proportional representation voting encouraged the political parties to carry on in the traditions of the old Imperial politics each fighting for their own narrow interests. If they agreed on policy at home, they fell out over foreign policy. They agreed on the need to free Germany of the Versailles Treaty but disagreed on the best way to do it. The DNVP would not work with the SPD, and the KPD would not work with anyone. Of the seven governments between 1924 and 1930, the longest lasted 21 months. One coalition government fell apart in a dispute over the style of the national flag! The largest party in the Reichstag, the SPD, disagreed amongst themselves about pushing the interests of the working class and

 'Women think about it'. A DDP election poster of 1928 reminds women of inflation, duty, wages, unemployment, rents and housing shortages.

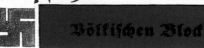 'The Wire puller'. A right wing nationalist election poster from 1924.

'Clean up the Reich'. A DDP election poster from 1928.

'First Bread then Reparations'. A 1924 Nazi election poster.

55

compromising with middle class liberals for the sake of the Republic and democracy. Of the Liberal parties, the DDP lacked clear leadership and the DVP, even under Stresemann, argued internally about the influence of big business on its policies. The Centre party found itself drifting to the right under Brüning. The DNVP, despite twice joining a coalition, was kept firmly on the Right in its hatred

60

of Weimar and Versailles and by Hugenberg, the newspaper tycoon. By the time of the Young plan it was working closely with the Nazis. The system of government merely coped. People became cynical of all the wheeler-dealing connected with making coalitions. The stability of these

65

years was a mirage.

Adapted from *Bismarck to Hitler: Germany 1890–1933*, G Layton, 1995.

4 The interpretation in Source D contrasts with the common view of Weimar Germany, 1924–1929. It deepens our understanding of Weimar Germany and why it should give way to the Nazis in the 1930s. Consider the following conclusions and find supporting evidence from the extract to back them up.

a Statistics can be used selectively to present a different picture of Weimar Germany in this period.

b The governments were not following sensible policies.

c The Weimar economy was not strongly based.

d Many people were actually worse off.

e Politicians did not support or believe in the Weimar system of government.

f The German people were put off the Weimar system of government.

g Politicians joined coalitions for selfish reasons.

h The recovery of Germany under Weimar was superficial and fragile.

3 What ideas are being used by the Right and Centre-Left of German politics to persuade the voters ?

5 *Weimar Germany and the Depression*

> We are sitting at the sick bed of Capitalism, not only as doctors who want to cure the patient but also as cheerful heirs who cannot wait for the end and would like to hasten it with poison.

Fritz Tarnow, trade union leader and SPD member, 1931.

Weimar Germany's economic revival in the 1920s was built upon the foundation of American money loaned under the Dawes Plan. Money that was needed and could not come from taxes had been borrowed by the Weimar Government. German companies borrowed from American banks to build new factories or to buy new machines to put in them. All of the money was invested in projects that in the long term would produce profits that would pay off the loans and the interest. What was needed was time.

Unfortunately, on the last Friday in October 1929 disaster struck at the heart of the American economy. A crisis of confidence on the Wall Street Stock Exchange in New York caused the price of shares to tumble. The shock waves from this disaster thundered all round the world.

The Wall Street Crash, 1929

The Wall Street Crash happened because Americans became frightened that the steadily rising value of their shares would not continue. Throughout 1929 share prices rose. Americans borrowed large amounts to buy shares because they could make more money from shares than the cost of the loan to buy them. Worries mounted throughout October. Could the rise in share prices keep going? Late in October nerves broke and some investors tried to sell the shares and take the high profits they had made. Other investors got wind of the rush to sell and joined in. The market was flooded with shares and inevitably prices fell. They didn't stop falling. Eventually some people lost the fortunes which, on paper a few days earlier, they seemed to be worth. They could not turn the shares into cash by selling them. Those who had borrowed to invest in shares had massive debts. They were forced to sell their possessions and their homes. American industry felt demand for their products fall and were forced to lay off workers. People stopped buying imported goods, German products amongst them. The banks which had lent money to American investors had little prospect of getting it back. In order to try to keep their business going the banks asked for their money back on other loans. The vast amounts that had been lent abroad were called back. So the economic crisis widened and deepened.

When foreign banks wanted the rapid repayment of their loans the German economy could not cope. Firms could not instantly find the cash so they went out of business. They sacked their workers.

Unemployment rocketed and so did the cost of unemployment benefits. Parties in the Reichstag were split over how to meet the bill. The SPD would not accept the increased contributions from the workers still in jobs or cuts in benefits that the right-wing parties wanted. The right-wing DVP would not accept tax increases. As a result, the political coalition formed after the 1928 election fell apart in March 1930. The Centre Party politician, Heinrich Brüning, was asked to form a new government. His idea of a 2.5% wage cut for civil servants was blocked by the SPD in the Reichstag. President Hindenburg backed his Chancellor and used Article 48 of the Constitution to decree the wage cut. The SPD challenged the decree. In this impossible situation Brüning asked Hindenburg to dissolve the Reichstag and hold a new election in September 1930. He hoped the electorate would back his sensible policies and a Centre-Right coalition. He could not have been more wrong. The results of the election saw a massive surge in support for the Nazis (see pages 11 and 38) making another coalition of parties even more unlikely. So President Hindenburg again used his powers under Article 48 of the Weimar Constitution to allow Brüning to rule by decree to solve the crisis. For the next two years Brüning tried to do this.

▲ An election poster from September 1930 showing Brüning as the last defence for Truth, Freedom and Justice in a Germany attacked by extremist forces

Das tote Parlament

DAS BLIEB VOM JAHRE 1848 ÜBRIG!
So sieht der Reichstag aus, der am 13. Oktober eröffnet wird.

Without the support of American money, Brüning set out to balance what Germany was spending with what she had as income. To make the two figures come closer together and balance out, he cut spending and raised taxes. The existing tax rates on things like income, beer and sugar were raised, and some new taxes were introduced. Brüning cut Government spending by reducing wages. Civil servants found their pay reduced by 23% by the end of 1931. Unemployment pay was slashed by 60%. These harsh remedies made the crisis deeper, and more businesses, even a major German bank, failed. German unemployment which had been 1,862,000 in 1928 shot to 6,042,000 in 1932.

'The Dead Parliament' 1930. A Communist criticism of the President's use of Article 48 of the Constitution to pass laws without consulting the Reichstag. On the President's desk are symbols of the Army, Business and the Church who now influence the President.

 A Nazi election poster from 1932 showing 'The Communist and the Guardian Angel of Big Business'

'Hitler – Our last hope'. A Nazi election poster appealing to the unemployed in 1932.

1 Explain how Brüning tackled the problems of the Depression in Germany.

The misery of the German people did not end there. Large land owners and farmers had been calling for help to protect their products from the competition of cheaper imported food. The Government raised the taxes or tariffs on imported food. This meant that the German people had to pay much higher prices for their food. Unemployment, expensive food and low wages caused widespread suffering and deepening desperation throughout Germany. Not surprisingly, Brüning was known as the 'Hunger Chancellor'. Of the population of 65 million in 1932, nearly 15 million Germans depended on social security or charity for their livelihood. Far more than in Britain or America, the Depression touched every family in Germany physically or psychologically. Germans felt a profound despair in the early 1930s that Hitler and the Nazis exploited.

Why did Weimar Germany fail?

The Weimar Republic was associated with the Versailles Treaty and its dishonour, which was helped along by the 'stab-in-the-back' legend. It had been disgraced by the French occupation of the Ruhr in 1923. The parliamentary system of proportional representation produced weak governments in a country with no tradition of democracy. In order to survive, the majority left-wing party – the SPD struck deals with the traditional sources of power and their influence on German politics continued in the life of the Republic. In the early years Weimar was troubled by problems of law and order and revolts from left and right-wing groups. Throughout its life Weimar had few real supporters. At the end, Brüning's rule by decree was autocratic. Hitler inherited this, and was the last person to fight to restore democracy. Economically Weimar Germany was saddled with the war debt and reparations. The period of inflation in the early 1920s created insecurity and suffering amongst all classes which they did not easily forget. The Dawes and Young Plans, whilst practical solutions, made Germany's recovery depend on foreign money. When the Wall Street Crash launched the world into Depression, it also pushed the already shaky German economy over the edge. German democracy and government was not robust enough to stand the measures taken to cope with the Depression and further alienated the majority of Germans. It is understandable that they should look for alternatives which the Nazis were all too ready to offer.

FOR DEFENCE ONLY.

GERMANY. "I NEVER DID LIKE THE LOOK OF THAT OLD WORD"

B The British magazine, *Punch,* comments ominously on German militarism in 1932

2 Study Sources B–E. They represent parts of the story of the Weimar Republic and its problems. Write an explanation for each one and its contribution to the failure of Weimar.

3 What were the other factors that contributed to the failure of Weimar?

 D The signing of the Treaty of Versailles, 28 June 1919

C 'Paper money! Paper money!, Bread! Bread!' A German cartoon, June 1923.

Papiergeld! Papiergeld!

„Brot! Brot!"

Juni 1923

'Hands off the Ruhr', January 1923 **E**

Hände weg vom Ruhrgebiet

6 *H*itler and the growth of the Nazi Party 1919–1929

The victor will never be asked if he told the truth.

Adolf Hitler.

With the war over, Adolf Hitler returned to Munich. The army gave him the job of spying on a small political party that might be of use to them for spreading nationalist ideas. The party, called *The German Workers' Party,* was founded by Anton Drexler and a journalist, Karl Harrer, in January 1919 and had about 40 members. It was not an impressive first meeting that Hitler attended in a Munich beer cellar on 12 September 1919. Hitler's furious reply to the suggestion that Bavaria should become independent of Germany won him admiration and an invitation to join the Party's committee. Adolf Hitler had found a purpose in life. In 1920 he was put in charge of the Party's propaganda. At the start of April 1920 he finally left the army and devoted himself to the Party.

The Nazi Party takes shape 1920–1921

- A new name – *The National Socialist German Workers Party.*
- A new symbol – the *swastika.*
- A new flag.
- A new 25 point manifesto or programme.

● Hitler takes overall control with a new title – *Der Führer.*
● The first 'strong arm' squads were formed of mainly former soldiers or *Freikorps*, this was the core of the S.A. (*Sturmabteilung* – Stormtroop). They would be the muscle of the new party, guarding their own and disrupting the meetings of others.

● Hitler bought a weekly newspaper – *Völkischer Beobachter,* partly with the help of a local army captain, Ernst Röhm, who used secret army funds.
● The first mass meetings were advertised and held.

Research
1 What were the important events in Adolf Hitler's life before 1918?

Despite being banned in nearly every state in Germany after the assassination of the Foreign Minister, Rathenau, the Nazi Party was allowed to continue its open meetings and the violence towards its opponents in Bavaria. Here it had the special support of the army and because of that the right-wing State Government, under Gustav Kahr. Hitler and his Nazi Party began to carve out a fearsome reputation for itself in Bavaria.

In August 1923 Gustav Stresemann's new Weimar Government took over in Berlin. It acted quickly to solve the crisis in the Ruhr. It ended the policy of passive resistance to the French and began reparations payments again. The Weimar Government in Berlin then cracked down on right-wing groups like the Nazis. The Bavarian State Government was told to ban the Nazis' newspaper *Völkischer Beobachter* for its attacks on Stresemann. Kahr refused. The Bavarian authorities appeared to have much in common with the Nazis and seemed to be on a collision course with Berlin. But then the Weimar Government took a hard line with the left-wing State Governments of Saxony and Thuringia; they ordered the Army to take control. This made Kahr and the army in Bavaria stop and think. They drew back from opposition or any hasty action. Hitler, however, could not afford to let the opportunity go. He decided to take the initiative and create a situation where Kahr would be forced to join him. Hitler launched the Munich Putsch (see page 16). After the Putsch failed in 1923 Hitler spent his time in prison writing *Mein Kampf*. Although Hitler wrote another book in 1928 usually known as the 'Second' or 'Secret Book' which was not published until 1959, *Mein Kampf* was to contain the core of Nazi ideas and become the starting point for all their policies.

Adolf Hitler during his 9 months prison sentence in Landsberg fortress, Bavaria. Whilst serving his sentence for taking part in the Munich putsch, Hitler dictated his book, *Mein Kampf*, to his friend Rudolf Hess (second from right).

Hitler saw a person's race as the key to their purpose and destiny. He interpreted all human history as showing that race was the key to progress.

The perfect or master race (*Herrenvolk*) was Aryan; its opposite was the Jew. According to Hitler, Jews lived as 'parasites' feeding off the countries in which they lived. Hitler saw in Communism such as in Russia, a Jewish inspired conspiracy to take over the world and stop the German people achieving their destiny. Hitler wrote that the conquest of Russia would not only secure living space (*lebensraum*) for the German people but also destroy the Jewish-Communist threat to mankind. These beliefs combined with an iron determination to overthrow the Treaty of Versailles.

Hitler and the Nazis aimed to make Germany great again. They would restore national pride. All classes in German society must unite to achieve this aim. More than a party, Nazism was a way of life. Nazism was, therefore, above politics and other parties were irrelevant; they would be eliminated. The interests of Germany were above those of any individual or group of individuals. Any method could be employed to achieve German greatness. There had to be ruthless efficiency in organising the country and its resources; this was to be a totalitarian state. Loyalty to the leader had to be unquestioning, this was the *Führerprinzip* or leader principle. He alone knew what was best for Germany. Hitler's experience in the First World War had given him an admiration for military organisation and leadership. To him Germany's rightful position in the world could only be restored by war; the country would be organised along military lines to bring this about. To Hitler expansion by war and conquest was natural for an Aryan nation. Germany's destiny of greatness in the world would be for true Germans, other races, non-Aryans, were inferior and were destined to serve the German people.

'National Socialist – Or all our sacrifices were in vain'. A Propaganda poster from 1928.

These ideas brought Hitler only limited support in Germany. Before 1929 Hitler was little known outside Bavaria and without great political prospects. He refounded the Party in February 1925 and spent the late 1920s building it up. He applied the *Führerprinzip* to Party organisation. Responsibility for the Party in each region was given to a *Gauleiter* (regional Party boss) who was answerable to Hitler alone. Hitler encouraged the Nazis to form 'associated' organisations for other groups, thus there were Nazi organisations for doctors, students, teachers, craftsmen, and many other professions. The Nazis also perfected their identity through mass meetings and propaganda using badges, uniforms, flags, and regimented displays. Finally, their supporters carried out acts of violence against all who might oppose them.

Mainstream right-wing politicians only had a little success to comfort them, faced as they were by the economic recovery of Weimar Germany after 1924. The Weimar Republic's first President, the Socialist, Friedrich Ebert, died in 1925. In the election that followed, the parties of the Left could not agree on a candidate. The KPD would not support the Centre and Socialist candidate, Wilhelm Marx, so the right-wing wartime hero General Hindenburg was elected with 14.66 million votes. His presence gave influence to the right wing of German politics, as he took advice from the traditional sources of power like the DNVP and the industrialists. However, Hindenburg acted fairly towards the Republic and it was only when dealing with the crisis of the 1930s that his natural political tendencies emerged. In 1928 the newspaper owner Alfred Hugenberg took over Germany's Conservatives (DNVP) and with the Nazis, began a massive campaign against the Young Plan. It gave Hitler valuable publicity. Though the Young Plan was accepted by the Reichstag in 1929, the campaign showed the strength of right-wing opinion in the Weimar Republic.

The failure of the Right to make an impact was due to the improved economic conditions. Under Stresemann and backed by American loans, Weimar Germany was becoming more prosperous. More people were at least on the surface, contented with the Republic. What Hitler needed was some form of crisis to break. In October 1929 the first rumblings of that crisis were heard far away in New York

2 The following sources relate to the early history of the Nazi Party. For each source identify the event or idea that it refers to. Explain the importance of each event or idea.

Instead of working to achieve power by force, we shall hold our noses and enter the Reichstag against the Catholics and Communists. If out voting them takes longer than outshooting them, at least the results will be guaranteed by their own constitution.

Hitler speaking to friends in 1924.

'The Party'. A bronze sculpture of an Aryan male by Arno Breker (1900–1991) intended for the inner courtyard of the new German Chancellery in Berlin. In 1937 Breker became 'Official State Sculptor'.

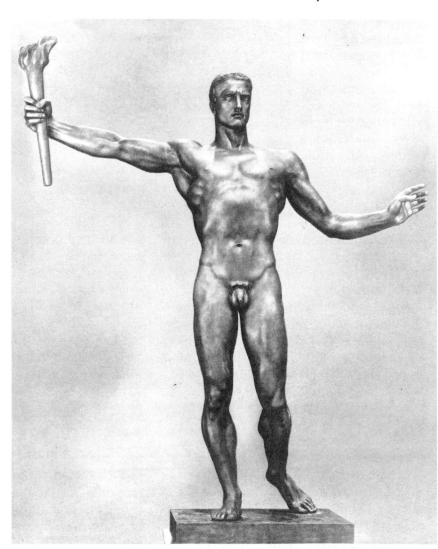

Point 3 – We demand land and territory (colonies) for the nourishment of our people and the settling of our extra population.

E

He meant to show the Conservatives how to conduct propaganda. The whole campaign was dominated by the Nazis. And for all this Hugenberg paid. Though it failed, three million who a year ago voted for Hugenberg were now won over to National Socialism.

A History of National Socialism, K Heiden, 1934.

G

G

Presidential candidates in April 1925 – Wilhelm Marx, Centre Party (13.75 m votes) above and left, Ernst Thälman, KPD (1.93 m votes)

Nazis in Bavaria in 1922. A mixture of flags, ages, soldiers and uniforms

F

7 The Nazi breakthrough 1929–1933

It is not consistent with the sovereignty of the State for a political party to keep a private army.

General Groener, Minister of Defence, urges Brüning to ban the SA, 10 April 1932.

In the September 1930 Reichstag elections, the share of the vote won by the extremes of German politics increased. The Centre Party kept much of its vote, the Communists (KPD) strengthened their support and the Nazi Party saw a dramatic surge in popularity. Their landslide success made them the second largest party in the Reichstag with 107 seats. Only the SPD had more. The Nazis were a real force in German politics but they had yet to become a real power. Because German politics had polarised, compromises and coalitions were difficult. For the next two years President Hindenburg used his Article 48 powers to allow his Chancellor, Brüning, to govern Germany by decrees. Brüning brought in his harsh measures to cope with the problems of the Depression (see page 24). With rule by decree, the Reichstag was not so important. This suited Brüning whose natural tendencies favoured a more autocratic, Imperial system of government. The SPD, alarmed by the success of the extreme right and left-wing parties, gave reluctant support to Brüning's policies. But this was not democracy, power lay with a select few surrounding the President. It was men like the influential Kurt von Schleicher, head of the German army (*Reichswehr*), who caused Brüning's downfall over the issue of the Nazi SA.

A painting from 1930 of an SA man during a fight

Since the 1930 election, the Nazi SA and the SS had made German life increasingly violent and unpredictable. In 1932 Chancellor Brüning had had enough. He decided to ban them. General Schleicher thought this unwise. He believed that it would leave the way open to the Socialists and the Communists. In his view the Nazis were a little rowdy but he sympathised

C 'Only the stupidest calves vote for their own butchers'.

He played on Hindenburg's fears that Brüning wanted to give away the land of bankrupt farms in Prussia to the unemployed. A scheme that had SPD approval. Schleicher stressed that the Nazi SA was the counter-balance to the Communists and Socialists. Encouraged by other right-wing voices close to him, Hindenburg soon had second thoughts about his ban on the SA. On 29 May Brüning was told by Hindenburg that he would not support him and Brüning resigned the next day. General Schleicher not only plotted Brüning's downfall but he also engineered a replacement Chancellor who in return for lifting the ban on the SA and the promise of a new election, would have Nazi support.

1 How do Source F and the anti Nazi sources (Sources C, D and E) show the differences between the Nazis' message and their methods?

with their approach to Germany's problems; to Schleicher the energies of the Nazis should be controlled and used. Schleicher was aware that support for the Nazis was growing. In March 1932 Hitler had challenged Hindenburg for the Presidency and received an impressive 13,420,000 votes against Hindenburg's 19,360,000. On 13 April 1932 Hindenburg signed an order banning the SA. General Schleicher worked behind the scenes to have the ban scrapped. He reminded Hindenburg that Germany's economy had not improved under Brüning.

 D

'Germany awake' was the Nazi rallying cry. It appears in this cartoon from January 1931 entitled 'The Forerunner of the Third Reich'.

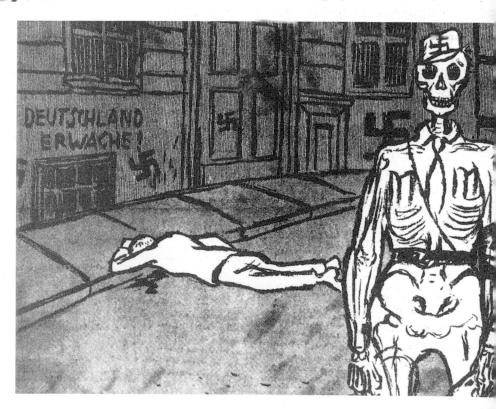

Brüning's replacement was Franz von Papen, another Centre Party politician with right-wing tendencies. He formed a 'Cabinet of Barons', so called because only one of its members did not have a title. His policies reflected the powerful farming and industrial leaders who backed him. On 20 July 1932 Papen illegally removed the Government of Prussia which had supported the Weimar Republic since 1918.

He reduced the rights of the trade unions. They and the SPD had little energy to respond and were soon faced with the July election Hitler had been promised. The election produced the largest vote for any one party ever recorded in Reichstag elections. It was a colossal triumph for the Nazis. They now had 230 seats in the Reichstag.

 An SPD election poster from September 1930 announces 'These are the enemies of Democracy'

 The Nazis appeal to women voters in this 1932 election poster. It reminds women of the millions of unemployed men, and children without a future, and asks them to 'save our German families' by voting for Adolf Hitler.

The police arrive after a fight between Nazis and left wing Germans. Increasing violence of this kind between 1930 and 1932 led to Brüning's attempt to ban the SA in April 1932.

The Nazis exploited their success with increased levels of violence against their political opponents. Members of the Government were attacked. Street battles with the Communists, deliberately provoked by the SA, were common. In the five weeks after the election in the state of Prussia alone 100 people were killed and 1,125 wounded. The fighting only added to the feelings of many Germans that the Weimar Government had lost control.

After the spectacular success of the Nazis in the July election, Hitler felt that he should be rewarded with the job of Chancellor but Hindenburg refused. Meanwhile Papen could see no support for him in the Reichstag and dismissed it, calling new elections for November 1932. In these elections the Nazis lost support. The number of Nazis in the Reichstag fell by 34. The runaway Nazi political machine seemed to have come to a temporary halt. This small setback did not stop Hitler asking to be made Chancellor again which was refused. The new Reichstag did not look as though it would support Papen any more than the one elected in July. Papen approached President Hindenburg with a plan. Papen wanted the new Reichstag

removed, martial law declared and a new Constitution made. Hindenburg could see some sense in this but changed his mind when General Schleicher told him that the army would not stand for it. On 1 December 1932 Hindenburg sacked Papen and made Schleicher the Chancellor.

General Kurt von Schleicher (left) and the new Chancellor, Franz von Papen, early in 1932

Papen was furious at Schleicher's scheming. Papen was determined to return to power. To achieve this he would use a coalition which included the Nazis. Papen gathered support from the right-wing of German politics, leading industrialists and the aristocracy. In this plan Hitler would get the job of Chancellor which he so much wanted but little else. That way the Nazis would be kept in their place. Only three of the eleven top jobs in the new government would go to the Nazis and then not the important ones. Papen would keep control of the army, trade and finance in the hands of other right-wing politicians he could trust. Finally, as further insurance against Nazi ambitions there would be a Vice-Chancellor with equal rights of access to the President. This would be Papen's job. Though Hitler had wanted more in return for his support, he was clever enough to see and seize the opportunity. The slight fall off in support for the Nazis in the November elections had made Hitler anxious. He only bargained for and got the post of Minister for the Interior for the Nazis. Otherwise he accepted the conditions of the coalition.

On 28 January 1933, Schleicher was sacked. Two days later, on 30 January 1933 Hitler and his government was sworn in by President Hindenburg.

The night of 30 January 1933 saw thousands of Nazis, SA and SS parade through the Brandenburg gate in Berlin to celebrate the appointment of Adolf Hitler as German Chancellor. Hitler, overjoyed, watched the triumphal torch light procession from a window of the Reich Chancellery.

Thus it was through the political intrigue and manoeuvrings of the powerful traditional interests in Germany that Hitler had finally achieved his dream of gaining legal power in Germany. However, the government that Hitler led from 30 January 1933 would need the support of other parties especially the Centre Party, for a majority in the Reichstag. Hitler wanted decisive power for himself and a Nazi majority. So he refused to co-operate with Ludwig Kaas, the Centre Party leader, and thus forced a new round of elections. These were due to be held in March 1933.

2   When did Weimar die?
    October 1929, September 1930, May 1932, July 1932, January 1933, or March 1933.

Who supported the Nazis?

Germans who voted for Nazis came from all levels of society and all regions, unlike most other parties. The Nazis had broad appeal and could claim to be the first people's party (*Volkspartei*). However they attracted some groups more than others. As one historian wrote, 'If the Party's support was a mile wide, it was at critical points an inch thick'. Protestant rather than Roman Catholic areas showed more support for the Nazis. Catholic loyalties were harder for the Nazis to break down. So too was Socialism in the industrialised cities.

Nazis gained more support in the countryside from farming communities which relied upon selling food and were most affected by the cash shortages produced by the Depression. In the residential suburbs the middle classes (*mittelstand*) sup-ported the Nazis. They seemed most threatened by the left-wing parties, had most to lose from social disorder and Communism, and felt let down by the Weimar Republic.

Many strong Nazi supporters were young. Of those who joined the Party before 1933, 41.3% were born between 1904 and 1913 yet they made up only 25.3% of the population. They were attracted by the vision of the Nazis and the prospect of being important and useful at a time of mass unemployment.

Nazi propaganda appealed to all with two important ideas. Firstly Hitler was a messiah figure who had come to save Germany. Secondly he would bring unity, to create a national community (*Volksgemeinschaft*) spanning class and social divisions

3   Read the following sources. Why did these people support the Nazis?

In 1930 the banks failed. All of a sudden, all credit was due. No one had any money. Everything gone. Do you know what that means? I own nothing. No money, no work, no food. Seven marks a week as unemployed. Families with two children, ten children and more, seven marks. And then came 1932. My mother and father went and heard Adolf Hitler. The next morning they told us what he had for goals, for ideas, how he was on the side of the unemployed. My mother wept for joy. My parents prayed dear God give this man all the votes so that we could get out of need. There was no one else who promised what he did.

Frau Mundt recalls the early 1930s.

Every person who thinks and feels as a German, the middle class, the farmer, the nobleman and the intellectual stands by Hitler. It is the nationalist movement.

Frau Solmitz, a teacher married to an army officer, describes support for Hitler, 1 June 1932.

All the students wanted to hear this man so admired by his followers and detested by his opponents. Everything about him was reasonable and modest, no shrieking fanatic in a uniform. He spoke urgently and with hypnotic persuasiveness. I was carried on by a wave of enthusiasm which one could almost feel physically. It swept away reservations. Here was hope, ideals, a new understanding, he spoke of the danger of Communism, the Jewish problem.

I joined the Party the next day. Some Nazi ideas were rough but I assumed they would be polished in time. I had to choose between a Communist Germany and a Nazi Germany since the political centre had melted away. I felt Hitler was moving in a moderate direction. In joining the Nazis I denied my upper middle class past. Like millions of others I was relieved of the need to think for myself.

Results of Major Parties (% of vote) in German General Elections during the Weimar Republic 1919–1933 (see also page 11)

Albert Speer recalls the first time he heard Hitler speak in January 1931 at the traditionally left-wing University of Berlin.

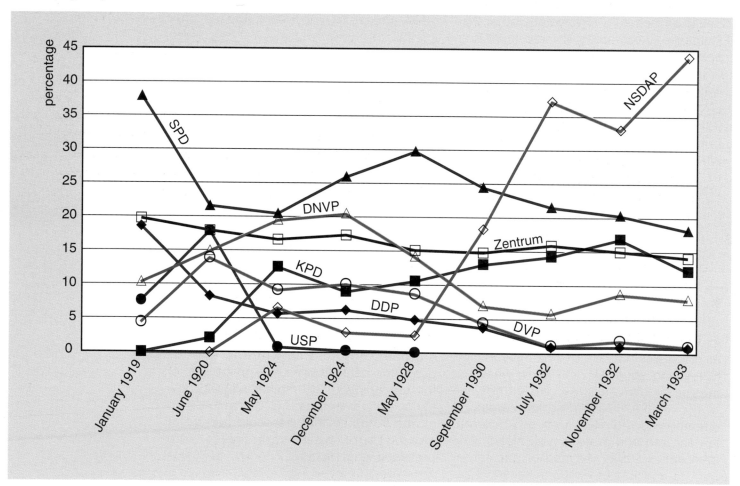

8 *H*itler and the Nazis tighten their grip on power

The other parties have had 14 years to prove their abilities. The result is a heap of ruins. Now, German people, give us four years and then judge us.

Hitler's Appeal to the German People, 31 January 1933.

The Nazis celebrated Hitler's appointment as Chancellor. Hitler had a position of power but not the total control he wanted. There was still opposition to the Nazis from the left-wing of German politics. The SA and SS set about eliminating it. They could be sure that the wave of violence they unleashed at their traditional opponents would proceed without police intervention. As part of the bargain with Papen, Hitler had chosen his Government posts well; the new Minister of the Interior, Wilhelm Frick, was a Nazi and he was responsible for the police. With elections planned for March 1933, the Nazis made sure that it would not be a fair fight. While the SA and SS harassed the left-wing parties through attacks on individuals and at meetings, Josef Goebbels, Hitler's propaganda chief, hammered home the Nazis' message. Hitler tried to frighten the Germans into voting for him with descriptions of what would happen in a Communist take-over. He, Hitler, should be given the power to stamp out the Communist menace. Then, on 27 February 1933, there happened what Hitler called, 'a God given signal'. The German Parliament building, the Reichstag, was burned down. A young Dutchman, Marinus van der Lübbe, a former Communist, was caught, tried, and executed for setting fire to it. The burning of the Reichstag offered a great opportunity to the Nazis. Hitler saw that he could use the fire to gain advantages in the forthcoming election. Immediately after the fire, Hitler and the Nazis persuaded the rest of the Government that Germany was under threat from the Communists. Such was the anxiety that Hitler whipped up, President Hindenburg gave him special powers. The day after the fire, Hindenburg signed an emergency law. the 'Decree for the Protection of the People and the State'.

Decree for the Protection of the People and the State, 28 February 1933	
Restricted free speech	Allowed imprisonment without trial
Restricted the freedom of the Press	Allowed mail to be opened and telephone tapping
Restricted the right to hold meetings	Allowed searches of homes and businesses
Restricted the power of the State authorities	Allowed confiscation of property

The Decree was approved by the Government as it was free to do in a national emergency. But there had been no real plot. The Communists were as surprised by the event as the Nazis but not as quick to react. News of the Decree spread through Germany and added to the confusion and shock caused by the fire. It seemed to convince people that there *had* been a Communist plot.

Hitler and the Nazis lost no time in putting their new powers to good effect. Truckloads of storm troopers went looking for their opponents throughout Germany. They broke into homes, seizing

Communists and Socialists. Back at the SA barracks or the local prison they were beaten up and tortured. Some were killed and their bodies hidden in woods or thrown into ponds. The offices of the Communists and SPD were wrecked, their meetings banned or disrupted.

▲ Leading Social Democrat politicians in Oranienburg Concentration Camp, shortly after their arrest in August 1933

Goebbels used his new powers to ban Communist newspapers and then extended the ban to Socialist ones. In Prussia, a State that made up two thirds of Germany, the Nazi Minister of the Interior, Hermann Goering, enrolled 50,000 SA men as police 'auxiliaries', they only had to put on a white arm band to instantly carry all the powers of policemen. Deprived of police protection, it is not surprising that over 50 left-wing supporters were killed and hundreds injured in the weeks before the election. Hitler enjoyed another big advantage before the election. Money was pouring into the Nazi Party from big business. What had been a trickle of cash before Hitler became Chancellor became a torrent afterwards. In a meeting with 20 industrialists on 20 February 1933, Hitler was promised 3 million Reichsmarks for Party election funds.

The election of 1933 took place in an atmosphere of intimidation and intense propaganda. The Nazis gained the support of 17.3 million German voters, an increase of 5.5 million on their November 1932 figure. Papen's DNVP could contribute 52 seats to add to the 288 that Hitler now commanded. It was a slender majority.

VOX POPULI
THE GERMAN ELECTION TAKES PLACE TO-MORROW

The first thing the Nazis did in the new Reichstag was to outlaw the Communist Party (KPD) which gave them a majority without DNVP support. Hitler was not satisfied. He wanted total power. He did not want to be challenged by the Reichstag or any other party. He moved quickly to complete his hold on Germany. On 23

 B

'The Voice of the People'. The *Daily Express* comments on the atmosphere surrounding the March 1933 elections in Germany. The Nazi Party received 43.9% of all the votes cast.

March 1933 the Nazis presented to the Reichstag, the *Enabling Act* (Law for removing Distress from the People and Reich). The law changed the German constitution. The *Enabling Act* did away with the Reichstag. If passed the law would allow Hitler and his Government to pass laws without reference to the Reichstag. The Reichstag was being asked to vote itself out of existence. Because of this, the *Enabling Act* needed to have the backing of two thirds of the Reichstag. This would only happen if the Centre Party voted for it. In the debate on the new law, Hitler turned on the Social Democrats, 'You, gentlemen, are no longer needed. I do not even want you to vote for the *Enabling Act*. Germany shall be free, but not through you.' Meeting in the new temporary home of the German parliament, the Kroll Opera House, the Centre Party voted with the Nazis and Nationalists for the *Enabling Act*. It was passed by 444 votes to 94. The Communists were banned from attending and 12 of the SPD had been arrested by the police. The remaining Social Democrats spoke out and voted against it. They were the only ones who did. Hitler now had the power he needed. Germany would become a dictatorship.

1 The following factors all played a part in establishing the Nazi dictatorship in 1933. Explain how each one contributed to the Nazis' seizure of power in that year.

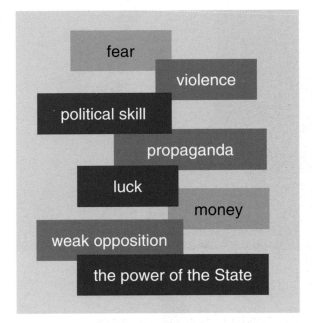

fear
violence
political skill
propaganda
luck
money
weak opposition
the power of the State

Why did the Centre Party support the Enabling Act?

Hitler made promises to the Centre Party about respecting the position and activities of the Roman Catholic Church in Germany. They were empty promises for Hitler but they reassured many in the Catholic Centre Party. Some in the Centre Party still hoped to co-operate with the Nazis in government. They were also aware that he had made some threats to the jobs of the minor civil servants, many of whom were Centre Party supporters. Some of the Centre Party may have believed that only decisive action like the *Enabling Act* would give enough power to the Government to restore Germany's pride. Hitler appealed for national unity.

Furthermore Germany had experienced the type of presidential government Hitler was proposing before, in 1923–24 and 1930. Many in the Centre Party assumed the *Enabling Act* would lead to the same system. And it was hard to resist the popularity of the Nazis expressed in the March election result. Hitler and the Nazis had the momentum of a large popular following. Some felt a sense of inevitability about the Nazi take-over. Only a small number, including Brüning, objected to co-operation with the Nazis.

Lastly there was no doubt that the Nazis' displays of massed paramilitary power before the crucial vote, sent out an unmistakable message. On the day of the vote the Centre Party may have been impressed or frightened by the presence of so many of the SA and SS shouting abuse, 'Centre pig', and chanting, 'We want the Bill or fire and murder'.

A-I-Z

ERSCHEINT WOCHENTLICH EINMAL • PREIS 20 PFG. Kč. 1,60
50 GR. 30 SCHWEIZER RP. • V. b. b. • NEUER DEUTSCHER
VERLAG, BERLIN W 6 • JAHRGANG XI • Nr. 42 • 16.10.1932

DER SINN DES HITLERGRUSSES:

Motto:
MILLIONEN
STEHEN
HINTER MIR!

Kleiner Mann bittet um große Gaber

C After Hitler's election success in July 1932, John Heartfield questions the real meaning of the Hitler salute and the claim that 'Millions stand behind me', October 1932

THE RED PERIL.

THE OLD CONSUL (to HITLER). "THIS IS A HEAVEN-SENT OPPORTUNITY, MY LAD. IF YOU CAN'T BE A DICTATOR NOW, YOU NEVER WILL BE."

D The British magazine *Punch,* on 8 March 1933, voiced fears about Hitler's ambitions

2 **a** What is the attitude to Hitler and the Nazis of Sources C–F
b How do they achieve their effect?
c What does the artist want you to think after seeing the picture?

E This Social Democrat cartoon from 4 March 1933 had the caption, 'Even when warm you may often be uncomfortable'

In Deutschland

ADOLF – DER ÜBERMENSCH

SCHLUCKT GOLD UND REDET BLECH

▲ The Nazi newspaper *Der Stürmer* published this cartoon in March 1932. The boy asks, 'Why must we freeze at home when there is so much coal?' and his father answers, 'because the hand of the Jew lies heavily on the people.'

F John Heartfield's picture from 17 July 1932 shows 'Adolf the Superman – He swallows gold and talks rubbish'

9 *T*he elimination of the opposition

> Measures taken on 30 June, 1 and 2 July to suppress the acts of high treason, are legal, being necessary for the self defence of the State.

Law passed on 3 July 1934.

With the power that the Enabling Act gave Hitler, the Nazis began to destroy or take-over any last source of opposition. The Nazis called this process *Gleichschaltung* which means 'bringing into line' or more commonly 'co-ordination'. It was a deliberate attempt to 'Nazify' Germany. People who were likely to disagree with the Nazis, such as Socialists or Jews, were removed from public positions. Only people whom the Nazis could rely upon would remain in important jobs. University lecturers, teachers, lawyers, and civil servants were sacked or worse. The SA who had intimidated their opponents so much in February and March 1933, revelled in their new freedom to terrorise. They used the first informal concentration camps, set up after the Reichstag fire, for prisoners of the *Gleichschaltung* whom they did not trust to the ordinary police. By 31 July 26,789 were held in these camps. The violence of the SA grew almost beyond Hitler's control.

The trade unions were an early target for the Nazis. The big unions were supporters of the Social Democrats. Back in 1920 the unions had great power. But by early 1933 they were weak. During the Depression they had lost both members and the will to resist. On 2 May 1933 trade union offices across Germany were occupied by Nazis. Their leaders were beaten up or arrested. The unions were merged into the Nazis' own labour organisation, the DAF (see page 86).

The political parties were also 'brought into line'. The Communists had been outlawed after the Reichstag fire, the Social Democrats were banned on 22 June 1933. Like the two small liberal parties, the DDP and DVP, the conservative DNVP disbanded themselves. They faced a falling membership and were 'encouraged' by the mysterious death of the DNVP Reichstag leader, Ernst Oberfohren, a man who had dared to criticise his party's continued co-operation with the Nazis. On 5 July, aware of its powerlessness and swept along by the wave of nationalist feeling, the Centre Party, too, disbanded itself. On 14 July 1933 there were no parties left to debate or oppose Hitler's 'Law against the Formation of Parties' which made the Nazi Party the only lawful political party in Germany.

Throughout Germany the State Governments were abolished by laws in April 1933 and January 1934. They were replaced by 18 Nazi Governors (*Reichstatthalter*) who had the power to make laws and appoint officials. Only Prussia, with its special place in German history and Goering's love of his role as its Prime Minister, kept its State Government. The Reichstag remained as a showcase for speeches and the ceremonial passing of special laws. In these ways by the middle of 1933 Hitler secured his position from any political threat in Germany.

Ernst Röhm, SA
leader, and Adolf
Hitler review an SA
display in June 1933

Socialists. Now some thought it was time for a 'second revolution' against the forces of the Right, the old traditional sources of power in Germany, businessmen, industrialists, and the army. Hitler's advisers said that many of the SA wanted the 'Socialism' in National Socialism to have a real and practical result. The SA expected some reward for their efforts; they wanted jobs, privileges, and a better quality of life. They threw their weight around and let everyone know their feelings. The SA mocked even the local Nazi Party officials calling them 'Christmas Tree Men' for their uniforms and 'political earthworms'. Their demands were already upsetting the industrialists and businessmen who supplied Hitler with the money to mount his expensive and impressive election campaigns.

Hitler now faced a potentially more dangerous challenge to his control of Germany from inside his own party. It came from the SA. They had been invaluable to Hitler in the 1920s and 1930s. In 1930, Ernst Röhm, an old friend of Hitler, was appointed leader of the SA to bring discipline to his private army. By 1934 the SA numbered about a million men and clearly had the ability to overthrow Hitler. Röhm and the SA seemed to be making demands that made Hitler uncomfortable. They rode the crest of a wave of violence and power that began in February 1933 and swept on through the *Gleichschaltung*. The SA believed they helped win a 'first revolution' against the forces of the Left, Communists and

A recruiting poster for the SA produced in September 1934, after the Night of the Long Knives

The SA's noisy suggestion that they be integrated into the traditional army caused anger and indignation in the elite officer corps of the army. The prospect of being put under Röhm's command was horrific. To have their traditions and status diluted by crude street fighters and men from the ranks would be a disaster. To add to this, the SA were coming into direct conflict with the army. The SA found it difficult to drop the terror tactics that helped bring Hitler to power in the 1930s. They still used their auxiliary police positions to persecute those they saw as their enemies. They flouted the conditions of the Versailles Treaty with regard to weapons and the de-militarised zone of the Rhineland, something that the army had been careful to observe, at least in the West.

Hitler needed the support of the army. The army were a part of the coalition of traditional power that lay behind the politics of Weimar Germany. They had been good to Hitler by not intervening at crucial points in his rise to power. The army officers were still a powerful force in German life and Hitler needed them to achieve his final glory, the powers of President, which the old and ill Hindenburg still held. More than that, Hitler needed the skill of the army officers if he was to achieve his long term aims of expansion beyond Germany's borders. The leadership and abilities of the SA thugs would be no substitute for experienced army commanders on the battlefield. Hitler was encouraged to see Röhm and the SA's activities in a threatening light by other leading Nazis like Himmler and Goering. They played up the ambitions of the SA because it suited their own wish for more power in the Nazi regime. Himmler as leader of Hitler's personal bodyguard, the SS, was officially a part of the SA and therefore under Röhm's command. This he resented.

Provocations and accusations increased the tension between the SA and the regular army throughout June 1934. On 29 June Hitler decided to act to nip the SA problem in the bud. He called a meeting of the SA leaders at Wiessee near Munich for the next day. The army and the SS were put on alert. Hitler flew to Munich and early in the morning personally woke Röhm and arrested him at gun point. Röhm was taken to Stadelheim Prison. The code word *Kolibri* – hummingbird – sent by Hitler to SS units throughout Germany, started the systematic arrest and murder of the SA leaders. On Sunday 1 July 1934, two SS officers sent by Hitler were taken to Röhm. They gave him a pistol and told him to shoot himself, promising to return in ten minutes. When they came back Röhm stood defiantly by his bed. Taking aim from the door one of the SS officers shot him through the throat and then finished him off with a bullet through the forehead as he lay on the ground. Hitler did not miss the opportunity to settle some old scores. Kurt von Schleicher, the last Chancellor of Germany and Gustav von Kahr who had double crossed him in 1923 and now aged 73 were killed. In all over a hundred SA leaders and important non-Nazis were executed. Even Von Papen was arrested but later released.

Reichsfuhrer-SS Heinrich Himmler taking part in a parade in Munich, 1938. In the centre behind him, is his deputy and head of the RSHA, Reinhard Heydrich.

This picture appeared in German newspapers in late June 1934 at the request of the Propaganda Ministry. It shows the SA man (bandaged) and the SS man as friends in their devotion to the Führer. What was the publication of this photograph meant to do?

The *Daily Herald* on 3 July 1934 comments on Hitler's actions in the Night of the Long Knives. What point does the cartoonist make?

A month later, on 2 August 1934, President Hindenburg died. No new President was appointed. The powers of the President were joined with those of the Chancellor, Adolf Hitler. The army swore an oath of loyalty to the Führer. They had not been passive in the 'Night of the Long Knives' as the ruthless destruction of the SA leadership became known. The army supplied weapons and vehicles to the SS execution squads and made preparations to counter any SA backlash. But with their leadership ripped away the SA went quietly, there was no backlash. The rank and file SA got the message and contented itself with rallies and demonstrations. Now there would be no 'second revolution'. The SS had established themselves as Hitler's main instrument of terror. Hitler had total control in Germany.

1 Why did Hitler order the 'Night of the Long Knives'?
2 What were the results of the 'Night of the Long Knives'?

THE STORM TROOPERS

> To interpret the law, judges should use the Party Programme, *Mein Kampf* and the speeches of the Führer.

Judge Rothenberger, a Nazi, writing in October 1935.

After 1933 the Nazis made Germany a 'police state'. This meant that the police had the power to act as they thought right and arrest anyone without trial. The back bone of the Nazi police state was the SS (*Schutzstaffel – protection squad*).

The SS was created in 1925 as Hitler's body guard. In 1929 their new leader, Heinrich Himmler, was determined to make them into an elite, formidable force. In 1930 the SS were separated from the SA with different uniforms. Himmler could see a new role for the SS. They became the Nazi Party's internal police force, responsible for finding and removing

Before and after the Night of the Long Knives, the SA played an important role in the Nazi police state. Here the SA act as auxiliary policemen rounding up suspected Communists in 1933.

anyone disloyal to Hitler. Himmler recruited only those who could prove their Aryan ancestry, physical suitability, and their loyalty. SS members tended to be better educated and from the middle classes.

The SS gave unquestioning obedience to the Führer. They saw the world simply as divided into friends and enemies. Their job was to search out and destroy those enemies – Communists, Jews, criminals, or homosexuals, anyone who undermined the 'national community'. To gather information about their enemies and to spy on traitors, inside and outside the Nazi Party, Himmler created the SD (*Sicherheitsdienst*) in 1932. He appointed a young naval officer, Rienhard Heydrich as its head. Heydrich spent 1932 recruiting mainly university graduates as agents in the SD.

In April 1933 Himmler was given responsibility for all political police in Bavaria by Hitler. Himmler's ambition was to control the security forces throughout the Reich. His rival for control of Germany's police forces was Wilhelm Frick, the Interior Minister. By early 1934, with the help of Heydrich's SD, Himmler had gained control of the political police in all the States of Germany except the most important, Prussia. For some time Frick had been trying to get control of the Prussian political police, the *Gestapo* (*Geheime Staatspolizei*). This was resisted by Goering who guarded his power in Prussia. Goering wanted Himmler as an ally against Frick so he appointed Himmler 'Inspector of the Gestapo' on 20 April 1934. Goering soon found that the SS were a formidable, independent organisation, that spread its influence throughout the Gestapo. Goering and his officials were powerless to stop it. This increase in Himmler's power meant that he inherited responsibility for the first concentration camp at Dachau, near Munich. From June 1933, with brutal efficiency, Theodor Eicke made Dachau the model for all future Nazi concentration camps. For those opponents of the Nazis who were detained there in 'protective custody' (*Schutzhaft*), it was a regime of terror run by the Death's Head

Units (*Totenkopfverbände*) of the SS.

Only Frick stood in the way of Himmler's ambition. The actions of the SS upset and challenged the Interior Minister's authority. Frick appealed to Hitler for support. But a compelling case for Himmler was made by the actions of the SS in the 'Night of the Long Knives' (see page 44). Himmler had demonstrated his absolute loyalty and the value of the SS as a ruthless weapon of power. On 17 June 1936 Hitler rewarded Himmler with sole authority over the police in Germany.

As *Reichsführer SS*, Himmler controlled a massive police machine. Its security organisation, the RSHA (*Reichssicherheitshauptamt*), led by Heydrich from 1939, included the Gestapo, the SD, and criminal police forces. Himmler also created his own armed

A recruitment poster for the *Waffen-SS*. New recruits had to be over 17 years old.

forces, the *Waffen-SS* (armed SS). From three divisions in 1939, the *Waffen-SS* grew to 35 in 1945, rivalling the power of the army. The concentration camps were run by the SS in a savage and inhuman manner. As the German army expanded the borders of the Reich, special SS squads policed the new areas removing opposition and those people they considered inferior or undesirable. The SS set up businesses and built factories to exploit the potential of these new lands and a limitless supply of slave labour. By the end of the war, the SS controlled a commercial empire of over 150 firms which made building materials, clothing, furniture, weapons, and extracted raw materials. Indeed from 1941, the function of the concentration camps changed as their economic value to the Nazi war effort became paramount.

The SS empire run by Himmler has been described as a 'state within a state'. Not only did the brutal and repressive hold on German society keep the Nazis in power but the economic and military influence of the SS grew. It became the major force in the Third Reich.

1 Why did the power of the SS increase?

What was the Nazi police state like for most German people?

In 1965 W.S. Allen, an American historian, published a pioneering book about the rise of the Nazis from his research in the small German town of Northeim. Inspired by a regional study of Nazism written by a British historian in 1971, Allen went back to the Northeim area to investigate the regional records of Lower Saxony. He had always regretted that the records of the Nazi Party in Northeim had been destroyed at the end of the war. In the State archives in Hanover, Allen found to his delight, uncatalogued and largely ignored, the carbon copies of all the correspondence of the Northeim Nazi Party from 1929 to 1938. As he wrote, 'This material would not only justify but require a revision of my book'.

Local Nazis parade through the centre of Northeim. This picture appeared on the cover of W.S. Allen's book.

Occasionally someone was released from the nearby concentration camp. Some idea of camp life must have got back to the people of Northeim. For the purposes of creating a climate of terror, vague knowledge was probably most effective. Press reports made it clear that if the Nazis were after someone, they would get him one way or another. A worker was sent to prison for 'insulting a police officer', a woman beggar for 'spreading political rumours'. By mid summer 1933 the Northeimers had a good idea that to express oneself against the new system was to invite persecution. Their own awareness strengthened the system every time someone cautioned his friend or neighbour. A teacher remembers a mother complaining about the book burning. He agreed with her but also warned her not to tell others in case she got into trouble. Late in 1933 several local Nazis organised an 'intelligence troop' of informers to spy on suspicious neighbours. It was unnecessary for the Nazis to suggest that someone who had no swastika flag buy one. The woman next door took care of that by cautioning her neighbour, 'letting her in on what one had to do'. Word spread quickly of Dr. Ruhmann who had imitated Hitler's way of speaking at a party one night and was reported by his hostess to the Nazis the next morning, 'Social life was cut down enormously – you couldn't trust anyone anymore'. In Northeim anyone not giving the Nazi salute as a greeting was considered to be reckless.

Those who had sworn resistance made excellent examples for the Nazis. A Socialist, Benno Schmidt, was given the dirtiest jobs at work. He was pestered to join the SA. His flat was raided. He was fined for petty things. His fellow workers refused to speak to him and finally beat him up. Schmidt left Northeim to work on the autobahns. Others suffered the same fate, thrown out of their job, given no unemployment pay, arrested, questioned, forced to sign statements, and threatened with the concentration camp. The example was seen by others. Social Democrat leader, Carl Querfurt was denounced in speeches. His tobacco shop was threatened, boycotted and his house 'guarded' by the SA. Finally Querfurt confronted the local SA leader, Ernst Girmann, whom he knew from childhood, 'I know why you've got a storm trooper guarding my back gate. One of these nights you'll throw a weapon over the wall and the police will "find" it the next day. You know that dog I have? Tomorrow night at 8 I'm going to let him out for exercise – out the back gate. I'll feed him at 9 if he's still hungry.' The SA guard was removed.

Hermann Schulze was sacked from his job on the railways for membership of the SPD and the *Reichsbanner* (an SPD paramilitary group). Denied unemployment pay, Schulze survived by doing jobs on peasant farms, being paid with food. All the time he was hounded by the local Nazis and the Gestapo. His house was regularly searched, mattresses cut open, walls knocked down and he was questioned at least twenty times. The peasants, afraid to be thought of as helping a Socialist, stopped giving him work. He went to work in the quarry, breaking stones. Finally in the winter of 1934 an unknown man knocked at his door in the cold and the rain and asked for help. He was a *Reichsbanner* man on the run from the Gestapo he said. 'Could Schulze help?'. He wanted to know of other *Reichsbanner* men in the area. 'Did Schulze have any weapons?'. Schulze said 'No' to all the questions and added, 'I'm through. I've had the stuffing kicked out of me. All I can do is put you up and feed you, which I'd do for any human being on a night like this.' When he came to leave in the morning, the man went to the door, looked back at Schulze, turned back his lapel and showed Schulze an SS button. Then he left without a word.

Adapted from the revised edition of *The Nazi Seizure of Power – The experience of a single German town 1922–1945*, by W S Allen, published in 1984.

2 Study Source B. How did the Nazi police state influence the behaviour of its citizens?

3 Why was the Nazi police state so effective?

4 Why did Schulze's visitor show him the SS button?

11 *T*he Nazis and propaganda

> To unleash volcanic passions, outbreaks of rage, to set masses of people on the march, to organise hatred and despair with ice cold calculation.

Goebbels describes his task in February 1929.

Propaganda is the organised spreading of ideas and information which is meant to make people think or act in a certain way. Hitler and the Nazis were experts at propaganda. In *Mein Kampf*, Hitler said what made for good propaganda. It had little to do with the truth unless it favoured the Nazis. It concentrated on simple messages and repeated them frequently. Propaganda was better if heard rather than read. For this reason the Nazis liked mass meetings, preferably held at night when Hitler believed people would be more easily persuaded.

Josef Goebbels was responsible for putting Hitler's ideas about propaganda into practice. He had proved his talent for propaganda during the election campaigns between 1930 and 1933. On 13 March 1933 Goebbels took charge of the new 'Reich Ministry of Popular Enlightenment and Propaganda' which had complete power over official information and German culture (see page 57). Goebbels did not have to persuade Germans to vote for Hitler now. He had to prevent anything critical of the Nazis being said or written and make sure that German radio, newspapers and the Arts all displayed Nazi ideas.

The most important new tool of Nazi propaganda was the radio because Hitler believed it reached the German people directly. The Nazis set up factories to build cheap radios like the 'people's receiver' (*volksempfänger*) which cost only 35 RM. They made sure that the new radios had a

Josef Goebbels, Propaganda Chief, broadcasts to the German nation

Ganz Deutschland hört den Führer mit dem Volksempfänger

▲
A Propaganda Ministry poster announces, 'All Germany hears the Führer with the People's Receiver'

and approved the programmes.

It was not so easy for the Nazis to control German newspapers. There were over 4,700 daily papers in 1933 and they were owned by many different people and organisations. The Nazis set about gaining control of Germany's newspapers and what was written in them. Their first target was the newspaper owners. They used the Nazi Party's own publishing company, *Eher Verlag*, to gain ownership of the newspapers. Socialist and Communist papers were taken over or destroyed. Middle class papers were pressurised into selling to the Nazis. On 28 June 1933, Max Amann, the head of *Eher Verlag*, became the leader of the German Publishers Association. The publishers had hoped his appointment would avoid further Nazi interference in their businesses. But on 3 October 1933 the Nazis passed the 'Editors' Law' which reduced the power of the newspaper owners and gave the editors responsibility for what went into the newspaper. On 15 November Amann took charge of the newly created Reich Press Chamber. It had powers to close down publishing companies that the Nazis considered to be unsuitable or unfriendly to them. Throughout 1935 and 1936 Amann used these powers to end, merge or take over the publication of nearly 600 newspapers. In 1932 Nazi newspapers were 2.5% of the total circulation. By 1939 *Eher Verlag* owned two thirds of the German press.

At the same time as the Nazis attacked newspaper ownership, the Propaganda Ministry told the journalists what to write and how to put it across. News had to come from only one source, the State owned press agency – the DNB. Daily press briefings were held at the Ministry where journalists were told how detailed articles should be, how events were to be treated, and even the size of the headlines. The journalists organisation, The Reich

limited range so that they would only pick up the German stations that the Nazis controlled. By 1939 70% of German households had a radio, which was three times the number in 1932 and the highest percentage of any country in the world. Broadcasting was directed at public places. Loudspeakers were put up in factories, cafes, offices, restaurants, even in the streets. The Propaganda Ministry was staffed by the keenest young Nazis, who produced the news broadcasts for the radio

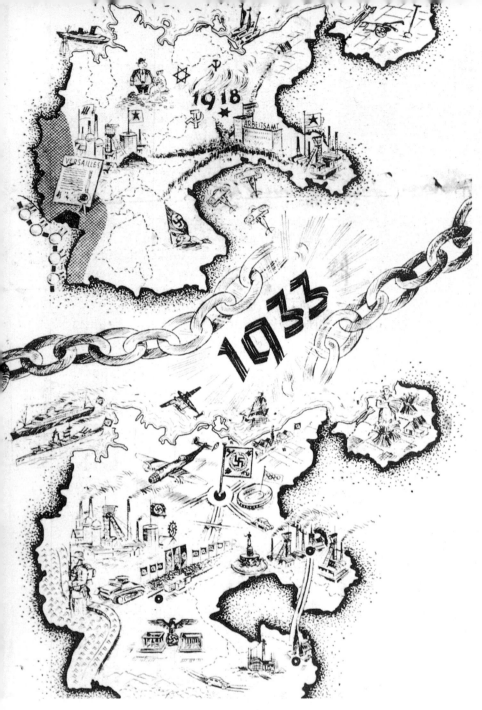

Association of the German Press, elected the Nazi Press Chief, Otto Dietrich, as their President on 30 April 1933. He made rules about who could become a journalist. By 1935 1,300 'Jewish and Marxist' journalists had been removed from their jobs.

As well as controlling the reporting of news, the Nazis created new public celebrations such as rallies, marches and rituals. The Nazis encouraged Germans to use the *Heil Hitler* greeting, the Nazi salute, wear military style uniforms and popularised the *Horst Wessel* song.

Goebbels made sure that the Press gave these events maximum publicity. None received more attention than the spectacular annual Party rally in Nuremberg. Everyone was expected to join in the celebration of these important days. Failure to take part, to listen to the speeches, to hang out flags would mark a person out as suspect and unreliable. As a punishment they might lose promotion, State benefits or worse.

1 Why would the Nazis want people to celebrate the events in the table below? You will need to refer to other chapters to explain fully.

◀ Nazi propaganda from a German newspaper, *Westfälische Landezeitung* in January 1939. How does it show Germany to have changed since the Nazi take-over of power?

Event	Date	Activities
Day of the seizure of power	30 January	Mass torchlight processions
Anniversary of the re-founding of the Party, 1925	24 February	
Heroes' Remembrance Day	First Sunday in March	Celebrated heroism
Führer's Birthday	20 April	Mass parades
National Day of Labour	1 May	Celebrated the 'national community'. Workers and employers paraded together
Mothering Sunday	Second Sunday in May	
Day of the Summer Solstice	21 June	
Day of German Culture	Second Sunday in July	
Reich's Party Day	September	A week's rally in Nuremberg
Harvest Festival	October	Peasants celebrate 'Blood and Soil'
Remembrance of Munich Putsch, 1923	9 November	Commemorates those who died in the Munich Putsch

▲ Nazi Party rallies at Nuremberg were often filmed by the Propaganda Ministry. This display on 14 September 1936 honours the German army.

My mother always went into Jewish stores. Once I went in with her, past the uniformed SA men on each side of the door. When we came out they did nothing. They didn't write down our names. In Marburg the mood was very pro-Hitler. You couldn't say anything on the street. There was something called the German look (*Der deutsche blick*). You looked over each shoulder and behind before you spoke. You had to wait and see with people whose politics you did not know.

I was in Hanover on the day that Hitler's motorcade drove by. From an open car Hitler waved to wildly cheering crowds. I noticed how such a mass of enthusiastic people saluted and threw flowers, that I was in danger of being pulled along. It infected you. And you think, could you be wrong and all the others right? I am also very much against the military but when I hear military music I get goose bumps. It was a danger though I didn't want anything to do with it.

There was a phrase Goebbels made popular, *Kohlenklau*, it meant 'coal snatcher', if someone left a door open someone would call, '*Kohlenklau*, close the door'. Everyone knew the catchy phrases. Against such clever psychology it was hard to defend yourself.

My mother ignored the orders to buy a large Nazi flag. It got very difficult. People would ring the doorbell and ask why haven't you hung out a flag for Hitler's birthday and so on. Eventually my mother bought a really small one.

Always my mother listened to foreign broadcasts which was strictly forbidden. One day a local Nazi leader came to our house and said that my mother ought to go to the Nazi evening meetings, and we had our dial set to an enemy station. My mother literally trembled that he'd look over and notice where the dial was set. But he didn't. He said if she was afraid he'd take her there and bring her back. She told me, 'I was more afraid of him than the dark.'

Anyone who could read a newspaper could work out what was going on with the Jews but some people did not read the newspapers. There was much I didn't know myself. I never suspected there were so many concentration camps, maybe two or three. I can believe there were many people who knew nothing or little. One knew the Jews had to work and afterwards they were taken to a camp but one could not imagine more.

Martha Brixius remembering life in Marburg in 1933.

2 Which parts of this account refer to the effects of propaganda and which to the effects of the police state? Explain your answer.

As well as creating their own art, the Nazis destroyed work they did not approve of. How is Gerstenberg's cartoon of 1933 critical of their actions?

How successful was Nazi Propaganda?

The Nazis did not use just the control of radio, and newspapers, and stage special events. The Nazis used the arts and leisure activities to get their message across and the young people of Germany were encouraged to be good Nazis through the Youth organisations and schools. The German people were subjected to a constant barrage of Nazi views. They were kept from hearing things that the Nazis did not wish them to know. The Nazis' propaganda was released into a society that was terrorised by the secret police, and undermined by rumours and suspicions. The Nazi idea of what was correct behaviour was then passed on at a personal level. It is hard to imagine what it is like to live in a society where only one point of view is publicly available. It is likely that people's ability to be critical was blunted. It is understandable then, that what people said and how they behaved would be what was expected of them. They would conform on the outside no matter what they believed themselves, in private. Without doubt the Nazi propaganda was important in supporting their hold on the lives of the German people.

3   Using all the evidence from this chapter, explain which type of propaganda you think would be most effective?

12 Nazi cultural life

Anyone who sees and paints a sky green and pastures blue ought to be sterilised.

Hitler's view on abstract, modern art.

A painting by Paul Padua entitled 'The Fuhrer speaks', 1937.

German nationalism and the superiority of the Aryan race. Through art the Nazis continued the cult of the Führer and a rejection of Christian values.

In music this policy involved the banning of performances of classical music by Jewish composers like Mahler and Mendelssohn. Jazz music was criticised as 'Negroid' and inferior, as was dance music because it was 'decadent'. German music had to be patriotic, military and popular.

In the theatre, as with music, only plays by traditional playwrights like Schiller, Goethe, and Shakespeare were performed because they were acceptable to the Nazis. In 1929 the Nazis set up the 'Militant League for German Culture', which organised protests and demonstrations against 'modern' art in all its forms. They staged a protest against Berthold Brecht and composer, Kurt Weill's new *Threepenny Opera,* and outside the anti-war film, *All Quiet on the Western Front*.

A photograph of part of an anti-Nazi mural by left-wing artist Diego Rivera, 1933, originally in the Rockefeller Center, New York

Under Nazi rule, cultural activities like art, music, theatre, literature, radio, and film all had to show Nazi ideas. The Reich Chamber of Culture was set up in 1933, supervised by the Propaganda Ministry. Its job was to make sure that all cultural activities helped mould the minds of Germans to Nazi beliefs. Under its influence the arts had to promote familiar Nazi ideas. They would be anti-Semitic and glorify war. The arts put forward ideas of

The Nazis burn books in Berlin, May 1933

1932. Instead, Germany's artists had to display realism, to be 'true to life', so that it was clearly understandable to ordinary people.

Only in the area of the cinema did the Nazis permit artistic work to go on which is still recognised as of high quality. The films of directors like Leni Riefenstahl are admired today. The German film industry established itself in the 1920s. Goebbels realised that film was an important media and an art form of growing popularity. He was clever enough to realise that if he used too heavy a hand in controlling the films that were made, the German public would be put off. However, Goebbels had the advantage that the people who owned the studios were Nazi sympathisers. Men like Alfred Hugenberg who controlled Germany's biggest film company, the Universal Film Company (UFA), were permitted to continue making films. Only 97 of the 1,097 feature films produced

No new drama came out under Nazi control. In 1935 the Education Ministry created the Schiller prize for the best new German play, but the judges found none good enough and did not award it.

Nazi Germany was no place for talented writers; men like Thomas Mann and Berthold Brecht joined 2,500 novelists, poets and playwrights who left Germany between 1933 and 1945. The action taken by the Nazis to burn books in Berlin on 10 May 1933 was a clear message to everyone. Goebbels organised the raiding of libraries and the seizure of books by writers who were not approved of, They were ceremonially burned. In 1936 the same thing was done to 5,000 paintings.

Art, both painting and sculpture, could not be abstract or modern under the Nazis. The most important development in German art at this time was the Bauhaus movement. It had started in 1919 and included artists like Schlemmer and Klee, amongst other architects, artists, designers, and sculptors who sought to unite all the different arts and crafts. The Bauhaus movement was centred on Berlin from 1930 but was closed down by the Nazis in

A still photograph from the film, 'Dawn', 1933. This tense submarine drama made by Hugenberg's UFA, celebrates comradeship and sacrifice.

 A still photograph from the film, 'Hitlerjunge Quex', 1933. The film tells the story of Heine who joins the Hitler Youth and while distributing Nazi Propaganda is attacked by Communists and dies.

▲ The opening of the Olympic Games in Berlin, 1 August 1936 from Leni Riefenstahl's film of the event

between 1933 and 1945 were at the request of the Propaganda Ministry. However, all scripts were checked by the Ministry. Directors and actors could not be Jews or opposed to the Nazis and, when the film was finished, it was checked again by the censors in Goebbels' Ministry. Whilst keeping a light control of the subjects for German feature films, Goebbels used film in a specialised way, to record large set piece Nazi political events. As well as this he closely controlled the cinema news film programme to ensure it showed the Nazi view.

Sport and physical exercise were a major part of the Hitler Youth activities. The major sporting event during the Nazi period was the Olympic Games in 1936. Hitler was determined to use it as an opportunity for propaganda. Leni Riefenstahl made a film of the Games. The Games saw some reduction in anti-Semitism (see page 63). Anti-Semitic newspapers were withdrawn, posters and signs removed. A few token Jews were allowed to compete for Germany. Opponents of the Nazis in Britain, America, and France tried to arrange a boycott of the Games. But the Games went ahead. Many spectators in the 110,000

crowd in the opening ceremony on 1 August were annoyed that neither the British nor American teams gave the Nazi salute. A few of the other foreign teams did. Hitler's enthusiasm for the competition and Germany's 33 gold medal winners was genuine. But his pleasure was spoiled by the success of the black American athlete, Jesse Owens who won four gold medals. For Hitler, Owens was descended from a primitive race with unfair advantages over civilised whites; Hitler thought they should not be allowed to compete. While the Games were on, every hospitality was given to visiting athletes and the impression made was very favourable.

More than 100,000 people crowded into the Olympic stadium, Berlin on 14 May 1938 to watch England play Germany at soccer. The English team, here in white, before the start of the game, won 6–3.

'Comradeship' by Arno Breker (see page 30). A relief panel for the triumphal arch in the centre of Berlin.

 'The Family'. A painting by Walter Willrich (see page 81).

Cultural life in the Third Reich was rigidly controlled. The best of Nazi culture was only mediocre; it had little free creativity or originality. In this sense Goebbels succeeded; culture could not be used for criticism of the Nazis. However, the Nazis did not succeed in using the arts to create a permanent Nazi outlook on life in the minds of the German people.

1 'The events organised by the Nazis in 1933 and 1936 clearly showed their approach to culture'. Explain this statement.
2 Study sources B, C, D, and E. For each source say what ideas the Nazis wished to convey.
3 How does each source convey the ideas?

 Architecture was the most important art form for Hitler. This was the grandstand at Nuremberg designed by Albert Speer.

13 *The Nazis and Christianity*

Hans Kerrl speaking to SA leaders in November 1935.

The ideas of the Nazis were opposed to the beliefs and values of the Christian Church. Nazism glorified strength, violence and racial superiority but Christianity taught love, forgiveness and respect for all people. The Nazis considered Christianity as the product of an inferior race, the Jews. This did not suit their ideas about the destiny and importance of the Aryans and the German people (*Völk*). Indeed the Nazis tried to introduce their own religious movement based on pagan ideas into Germany

Women in Bronze Age costumes celebrate a pagan Harvest Festival in 1933

However, whatever the Nazis believed deep down about Christianity, Germany was a Christian country. The influence of the Churches in German society, as Hitler knew, could not be ignored. Most Germans, about two thirds, were Protestants, whereas most of the other third were Roman Catholic. The Catholics consistently supported the Centre Party in German politics. Hitler aimed to remove the influence of the Centre Party (see pages 37 and 41).

With this in mind, Hitler came to an agreement, called a Concordat, with the Pope in Rome in July 1933. The Concordat offered religious freedoms of worship and education for German Catholics. In return, the Catholic Church agreed to stay out of politics. But Hitler had no intention of keeping his promises to the Pope. From the start of 1934 Catholics saw the true face of Nazi religious policy. Their priests were harassed and arrested, their schools interfered with and their youth clubs, like The Catholic Youth League, disbanded. The Catholic Church was weakened. In 1937 the Pope, Pius XI, made his disillusionment known in a famous statement, 'With Burning Anxiety' (*Mit Brennender Sorge),* in which he attacked the Nazi system. Nazi persecution of priests continued after 1937; many were put in concentration camps. In August 1941 Cardinal Archbishop Galen bravely criticised the Nazis for their abuse of human rights and their euthanasia programme.

German Christian students holding a meeting in Berlin in 1938

The German Protestant Church received no better treatment from the Nazis. There were some Protestants who admired the Nazis and wanted to see their Church under Nazi control. They were called 'German Christians' (*Deutsche Christens*). They were happy to see the process of *Gleichschaltung* (see page 44) applied to their Church. Their leader, Ludwig Müller, became the first Reich Bishop in September 1933. Changes like this angered other German Protestant ministers. They felt the conflict between Nazi ideas and the basic beliefs of Christianity. They were led by a strong critic of the Nazis and former First World War submarine captain, Pastor Martin Niemöller. In December 1933 they formed the 'Pastors' Emergency League' (*Pfarrernotbund*) for clergy who opposed the Nazis. Determined to have nothing to do with the Nazi 'German Christians', Niemöller and other *Pfarrernotbund* ministers started their own 'Confessional Church' (*Bekennende Kirche*) in October 1934. In this way they kept their Protestant faith and continued to criticise the actions of the Nazi regime.

However, by 1935 the Nazis' attempts to control the Churches had been partially successful. A Ministry of Churches was established under the leadership of Hans Kerrl. Church schools were abolished and, as with the Catholic Church, the Nazis

A poster critical of the Nazis' treatment of Christians, 'We go forward to pray'

aimed to influence young people by promoting the Hitler Youth rather than Church youth clubs. The Churches found it difficult to counter the press campaigns which aimed to tarnish the reputations of the clergy. Priests and ministers were arrested. Niemöller himself was sent to a concentration camp in July 1937, along with many other Confessional Church ministers. His Church was banned. Niemöller was freed by the Allies in 1945. Fuelled by the hatred of Christianity of several high ranking Nazis, like Martin Bormann and Reinhard Heydrich, and the confidence of early successes in the war, persecution increased after 1940. Monasteries were closed, Church property attacked and Church activities further restricted.

Apart from the Nazis' attempts to weaken traditional Christian faiths, they tried to supplant them with a religious movement of their own. It was based on an adulation of Hitler as a new messiah, a rejection of Christian values, ideas about the destiny of the German race and the use of modernised pagan ceremonies. This German Faith Movement did not receive much support from the mass of the German people.

The Nazis never destroyed the established Churches in Germany. They made it difficult for Christians to worship but the Churches remained open and services were held. However, Hitler succeeded in his aim of weakening the Churches as a source of resistance to his policies.

1 How did Hitler and the Nazis remove the Christian Churches as a source of opposition?

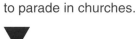
A memorial service for an SA leader in 1934. From 1935 the SA were not permitted to parade in churches.

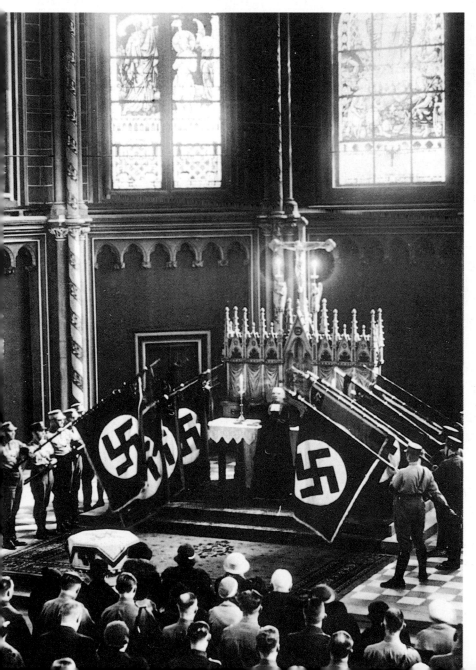

B

We demand a fight against unreligious and unpatriotic Communism and its Christian Socialist followers. The way to the Kingdom of Heaven is through struggles, the cross and sacrifice, not through a false peace. We see a living Christianity of action, rooted not in mere compassion but in obedience to the will of God and in gratitude for Christ's death on the cross. Mere Compassion is 'charity' and leads to complacency and effeminates a nation. We know about Christian duty and charity towards the helpless but we demand the protection of the nation from the unfit and the inferior. We see a danger from the Jews who bring foreign blood into our nation. We object to them having citizenship. The Holy Scriptures tell us of God's anger and self-denying love. Marriages between Jews and Germans must be prohibited.

Adapted from the ten points of *German Christians for an Evangelical Reich Church*, 1933.

C

I and the other nurses were part of a Bible reading circle in our Lutheran church. We did not like the German-Christian line of our minister. So we agreed to go to see Niemoller. I knew he had already been set upon and I wondered if he would get into trouble for seeing us. I can still see him in front of me now saying, 'Nurse Emmi, I must say as Luther did. Here I stand. I cannot do otherwise. God help me.' I belonged to his circle and we knew each other by face but not by name. I read a flyer by Niemoller on the first commandment, 'Thou shalt have no other God but me'. Niemoller said that the Nazis were trying to make a God out of Hitler.

Emmi Heinrich remembers meeting Martin Niemoller in 1934 while training as a nurse in Berlin.

Why did the Churches not resist the Nazis more robustly?

The Nazis were too clever to attempt attacking the Churches outright. This would risk upsetting large numbers of German Christians. The Nazis' policy was to wear the Churches down. This made it hard for the Church to fight back. Moreover many senior churchmen in the Roman Catholic and Protestant Churches were naturally conservative. Left-wing parties seemed to threaten revolution and Communism was atheist. Thus the Church would ally itself with an apparently more dangerous force if it came out against the Nazis. The Catholic Church was anxious to protect its position in German society. In 1870, under Chancellor Bismarck, the Catholic Church's influence had been attacked by the Government in what was known as the *Kulturkampf*. The Catholic bishops wanted to avoid a repetition of this policy. The Protestant Church was more closely tied to the German state and did not have the support of being a part of a world wide organisation like the German Catholic Church. It was also weakened as an anti-Nazi force because some of its members sided with the Nazis. Against the power of the Nazi state, with its organisation and ruthlessness, the Churches faced a formidable opponent.

Boys after confirmation into the German Protestant Church in 1933. This was forbidden by the leadership of the HJ after 1936.

2   Using all of the sources, why would many Germans have disliked the Nazis' treatment of the Christian Churches?

14 *T*he Nazis and the Jews

The idea of the racial enemy is as essential to National Socialism as the class enemy is to Communism.

From T Heuss, *Hitlers Weg*, 1932.

Adolf Hitler had an obsessive hatred of Jewish people and from 1933 he was able to use his power to persecute them. Anti-Semitism became Government policy.

On 1 April 1933 Hitler ordered a boycott of Jewish shops, doctors, lecturers and lawyers. On 7 April the *Law for the Restoration of the Professional Civil Service* was passed, which banned Jews from Government jobs. In May 1935 Jews were forbidden to join the army, so under Hitler, German Jews would not be able to serve their country as they had in the First World War. Throughout the summer of 1935, anti-Jewish notices appeared in shops and restaurants. Just before the massive Nazi Party rally at Nuremberg, Hitler introduced harsh new laws. On 15 September 1935, he passed the first of the so called *Nuremberg Laws*. The *Law for the Protection of German Blood and Honour* prohibited marriages between Jews and non-Jews. Any sexual relations between Jews and non-Jews outside marriage was a criminal and imprisonable offence. The second law produced on 15 September was the *Reich Citizenship Law*. It was confirmed by a decree on 14 November which clarified the problem of the *Mischlinge*, the quarter- and half-Jews. This law removed the rights of Jews as German citizens. They could not vote and the law made them 'aliens' or 'guests' in their own country. These laws paved the way for more persecution.

▶ B

Anti Jewish propaganda from a German children's book, 1938

Hitler had to reduce the level of anti-Semitic activity during 1936 when Germany hosted the Olympic Games. Restrictions on Jews were relaxed. Hitler did not want bad international publicity for his new Germany. Anti-Semitic signs were removed. Many Jews took the opportunity to leave Germany. However, after the Olympics and throughout 1937, the process of Aryanisation continued. This process aimed to squeeze the Jews out of all business life in Germany. They were banned from professional jobs in 1936. Pressure increased for Jewish firms to 'voluntarily' sell out to Aryan German firms. From 1 March 1938 Government contracts could not be awarded to Jewish firms. From 30 September, only Aryan doctors were allowed to treat Aryan patients. Attacks on Jews increased as the persecution became fiercer. On 17 August 1938, it was announced that all Jews had to use new names in their signatures, men added the name 'Israel' and women, 'Sarah', and from 5 October, their passports had a large red letter J stamped in them.

On 7 November 1938 a young Polish Jew, Herschel Grynszpan, walked into the German Embassy in Paris and shot the first official he met. Grynszpan was protesting at the treatment of his parents in Germany who had been deported to the Polish border and left to fend for themselves. The death of the official, Ernst von Rath, gave Josef Goebbels the opportunity to win favour with Hitler. He arranged a pogrom – an all out assault on Jewish property, shops, homes and synagogues. So many windows were smashed in the campaign that the events of 7–8 November became known as *Kristallnacht* (Crystal Night or Night of Broken Glass). About 100 Jews were killed and 20,000 sent to concentration camps.

Many Germans were disgusted at *Kristallnacht*. Hitler and Goebbels were anxious that it should not be seen as the work of the Nazis but as a spontaneous outburst of anti-Jewish activity by the German people. After *Kristallnacht* no one in Germany or the world would be mistaken about the Nazis' policy towards the Jews. Hitler officially blamed the Jews themselves for having provoked the attacks and increased his campaign against them. On 12 November he instructed insurance

Clearing up after *Kristallnacht*, 7–8 November 1938. Inset: Herschel Grynszpan.

companies to hand over any money due to Jews, for repairs to true Germans' property. The Jews were fined one billion Reichmarks as compensation for the damage caused. Jews would no longer be able to own, or manage any business or shop or employ workers. On 15 November 1938 Jewish school children were banned from ordinary German schools, they would have to go to Jewish schools. The process of Aryanisation was continued with extra enthusiasm by the Nazis. By 1 April 1939 nearly all Jewish businesses had been closed down or sold.

Hermann Goering had been happy to take Jewish money to support the German economy. But in the last few months of 1938 Goering's authority over the Jews was challenged by a more sinister source, the SS. Himmler had been issuing orders restricting the lives and movement of Jews in Germany. His wish was to eliminate the Jews completely from Germany. As Goering had achieved his goal of bleeding the Jews of their wealth, his interest in them declined. Therefore on 24 January 1939, he handed over to the SS the practical responsibility of removing them from Germany. This would be achieved by forced emigration, a policy followed successfully by Adolf Eichmann in Austria.

At this time the Nazis do not seem to have considered the mass slaughter of Jews; they merely wanted to rid Germany of them. They wanted other countries to take the Jews as refugees, and they even discussed a scheme to settle Madagascar with German Jews. With the outbreak of war, the persecution of German Jews increased. On 1 September 1939 German Jews were subject to a curfew. Later that month the Gestapo confiscated all radios from Jews. By March 1940 clothing and food for Jews was reduced.

The outbreak of war in September 1939 changed Nazi attitudes to the Jewish question in two ways. Firstly, it allowed more extreme treatment of the Jews without concern for world opinion. Secondly, the war increased the number of Jews under German control and removed the very areas which the Nazis had hoped

to use for the forced emigration of Jews from Germany. The 3 million Polish Jews were the most pressing problem. Unable to find a satisfactory way of moving on the Jews in the captured territory, the Nazis experimented with the idea of gathering them all in one place in 'Jewish reservations' or 'Reich ghettos'. During 1940 they organised Jewish ghettos in the cities of Poland, with Warsaw as the largest. Many Jews died from starvation in the ghettos. Close to the ghettos the Nazis organised labour camps. They did not

The shrunken head of a prisoner became the gruesome paperweight of an SS officer

mind how many of the Jews died doing this hard physical work without adequate food because there were many more to take their places.

With the launch of Operation Barbarossa, the invasion of Russia, on 22 June 1941, *Einsatzgruppen* (Special Task Forces) moved into Russia behind the advancing German armies to round up and kill Jews. Their orders made no distinction between Jews and Communists. Those

D

The *Einsatzgruppen* at work. A soldier shoots a Polish Jewess and her child as they run across a field.

Babies were a danger during a search. Crying could give everyone away. Their own mothers smothered them with pillows. A drawing by Ella Liebermann.

E

Ella Liebermann's family was expelled from Germany to Poland in 1938. Deported from a ghetto to Auschwitz-Birkenau, she survived because of her ability to draw. The pictures of her terrible experiences (Sources E, G, and H) were made in the years after her liberation in 1945, aged 17. Ella Liebermann lives today in Haifa, Israel.

picked out were marched to the outskirts of their villages, forced to dig their own graves and then shot. As the process continued, Jewish women and children were included in the executions. The numbers killed can only be estimated but by 1943 it is thought that the *Einsatzgruppen* had murdered 2.2 million Russians and Jews.

However the vast numbers of Jews in Germany and the newly occupied lands remained a problem for the Nazis. Due to the war, Heydrich, Himmler's deputy was having difficulty deporting so many Jews. In the summer of 1941 a decision was taken by senior Nazi leaders to seek a permanent and final solution (*Die Endlösung*) to the Jewish question. It is difficult to determine who was responsible

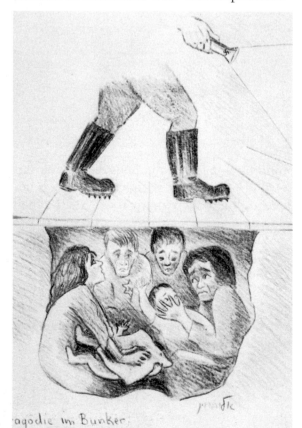

for the decision. Although Goering signed the order, the initiative seems to have come from Himmler and the SS with Hitler's approval. On 20 January 1942 Heydrich summoned senior officials to Wannsee, Berlin to discuss the Jewish problem. They decided to start the extermination of all Jews in German territory. The first extermination camp was built and began operating on 17 March 1942 at Belzec on the eastern Polish border. Many other camps in Poland, Germany and Austria followed. By the summer of 1943 Jews from all over German occupied Europe were being transported to their deaths in these camps.

American troops made German civilians bury the Jewish dead at Landsberg Concentration camp in 1945

1 Choose just three events which you consider to be the most significant points in the Nazis' treatment of the Jews. Explain why you have chosen them.

Research

2 Some people survived the Nazi death camps. They have given us valuable evidence of life in these camps. Find out what happened to the people who were sent to the camps.

Selbstmord als Erlösu

ACHTUNG
Hochspannung
Lebensgefahr

 F An execution at Auschwitz-Birkenau by prisoner 5826, 1944

 G Roll call at Auschwitz-Birkenau drawn by Ella Liebermann, a prisoner

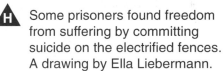 **H** Some prisoners found freedom from suffering by committing suicide on the electrified fences. A drawing by Ella Liebermann.

Why did Hitler want to persecute the Jews?

Hitler and the Nazis did not invent anti-Semitism. Hostility towards Jews was a long established tradition in Europe. It may be traced back to the Jews' treatment of Jesus. The Jewish community was easily identified in most German towns. They have a distinctive culture. Their respect for education often led to more of them having a 'privileged' position as doctors, lawyers or businessmen than non-Jews. In the late nineteenth century, anti-Semitism became mixed with racial and social theories of evolution gained from Darwin's work. This gave anti-Semitism a false respectability.

Hitler tapped into the anti-Semitic tradition in German culture. His own personal hatred of the Jews stems from his time in Vienna as a young man trying to make a career for himself as an artist. Moody and unpredictable, Hitler had the artistic temperament but none of the talent. He was rejected twice by the Academy of Fine Arts in Vienna. It was a deep shock to him. He lived a life little better than that of a tramp from 1909 to 1913 and they were the unhappiest days of his life. Hitler had a great interest in politics and he read anti-Semitic articles that were commonly in the newspapers of the day. In his own studies he picked up bits of philosophy, politics, and religion in random way. He had little money or success. He lived a hand to mouth existence. When he tried to explain his situation, he blamed the Jews, the priests, or the Social Democrats. But above all, as his thinking developed, the Jews seemed to be the main cause of all that was wrong with the world, not least of which were Hitler's own failures. To him this was a simple and exciting discovery.

A painting of the Parliament building in Vienna by Adolf Hitler

Why was Hitler able to persecute the Jews?

When Hitler began his political career fate fed him a set of circumstances that he could exploit, the 'stab in the back', the Versailles diktat, the political weakness of Weimar, and the economic problems of the early 1930s. Through his talent as a speaker he could unite all these problems with his anti-Semitism and produce a potent doctrine of hatred. He offered a simple solution to the complex problems that Germany faced.

Hitler did not set out to eliminate all Jews. The process happened gradually, each step made it easier for those involved to contemplate the next. At the start the Nazis wanted to remove all the Jews from Germany. This became more difficult as territory was won by the German army on the Eastern Front. From evacuating Jews the Nazis moved on to eliminating large numbers of Jews amongst the Russians they conquered. Gathering Jews together in ghettos which had appalling conditions and were often infected with typhus, seemed to provide evidence to support the Nazis view that Jews were diseased. The success they had killing Jews in Russia convinced the Nazis that they could succeed in a bigger enterprise – the systematic killing of all Jews.

There was little German opposition to these aspects of the Nazis' work because Hitler had been so effective in removing all opposition within Germany and placing Nazis in positions of power. Germans were subjected to a constant barrage of anti-Semitic propaganda. Some believed it. Of some things, Germans were simply not told. For many ordinary Germans who felt powerless to resist the persecution of Jews, they consoled themselves with the thought that this was the price they had to pay for all the other 'benefits' of Hitler's rule. Some of those Nazis doing the killing were psychologically disturbed and enjoyed the work. Others believed they were merely being organised and efficient in the way they followed orders and dealt with a problem.

15 The Nazis and young people

> He who serves our Führer, Adolf Hitler, serves Germany and he who serves Germany, serves God.

Baldur von Schirach speaking to Hitler Youth, 25 July 1936.

movements belonging to other political parties were closed down in 1933. Those of the Churches soon followed (see p.61). In their place the Nazis promoted their own organisations for young people. Under Nazi rule four separate organisations were developed which recruited girls and boys from the ages of 10 to 18. Boys joined the DJ – German Young People (*Deutsches Jungvolk*) at the age of 10 and moved on to the HJ – Hitler Youth (*Hitler Jugend*) when they reached 14. Girls joined the JM – League of Young Girls (*Jungmädelbund*) at 10 years old and then the BDM – League of German Girls (*Bund Deutscher Mädel*) at 14. Although an organisation for 18 to 21 year old girls was started in 1938

The Nazis believed that to control Germany's future they had to influence the minds of young people in Germany. They tried to do this through their Youth movements and the schools. Adults were harder to influence than children. They aimed to make all young people loyal Nazis.

Baldur von Schirach, leader of the Hitler Youth, was appointed 'Youth Leader of the Reich' on 17 July 1933. His job was to make sure that the Nazis gained control over all Germany's young people. This was part of the wider political process of *Gleichschaltung* (see p. 44). Youth

Hitler Youth are welcomed to a camp in September 1938, by their leader, Baldur von Schirach

 A BDM Propaganda poster

(*Glaube und Schönheit*) they were considered less important than boys because after 18, boys went on to military service in the army. The Hitler Youth movements developed from the Youth section of the SA.

The main purpose of the Hitler Youth organisations was to indoctrinate young people with important Nazi ideas and values, therefore duty, obedience, honour, courage, strength, and ruthlessness were stressed, whereas peace, kindness, intellect, individuality, and humanity were despised. Beyond that the boys were prepared to excel at military type activities and the girls for motherhood. Both girls and boys were expected to take part in appropriate physical training.

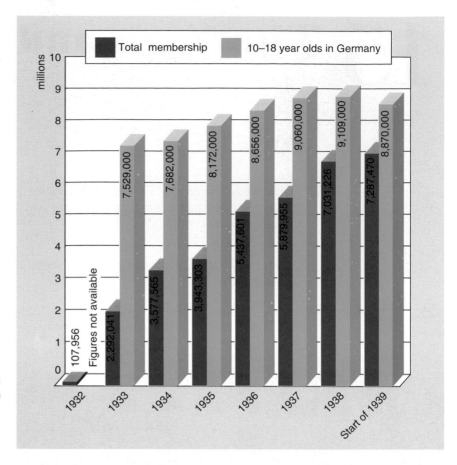

▶ Membership figures for Hitler youth movements 1932–1939

▶ Activities for girls stressed physical fitness, 1938

 HJ on a cross country run in March 1938

 The appeal of camping with the HJ is shown in this page from a children's colouring book

 HJ enjoy singing military songs, 1934

Many young people were attracted by the exciting and interesting activities of the youth movements. There were many outdoor events such as camping and hiking as well as sports. Some enjoyed the military aspects of the Youth movements, the uniforms, the marching, and the discipline. Other young people liked the music that was a frequent part of cultural activities or military parades. For some young people the chance to belong to something that seemed powerful and relevant to German life was important. There was great comradeship among the Hitler Youth and all the Youth groups were encouraged to do better at their training through competition with each other. In the lives of many young Germans the Nazi Youth organisations formed another point of focus apart from school and home for their attention and energies.

 11 year old boys in the HJ are instructed in shooting. In the background older HJ members are practising drill.

The *Hitler Youth Law* of 1 December 1936 confirmed this state of affairs. The HJ was given equal status to home and school. The law made it virtually impossible to avoid joining the Hitler Youth organisations. However young people might sign up but not be enthusiastic or regular members. There was no mistaking the intention of the *Second Hitler Youth Law* passed on 25 March 1939. This made membership of the Hitler Youth and the 'duty of youth service' to Germany, compulsory. Members of the Hitler Youth had to swear an oath of loyalty to the Führer.

The young people in Hitler Youth organisations were a valuable way of checking up on society. They kept watch on their parents and made sure they were behaving and speaking in a way the Nazis would approve of. The Hitler Youth would also keep an eye on their teachers. For young people this role appealed. It is normal for young people seeking their independence, to challenge authority. From within the Hitler Youth, they had a ready made justification. How much they enjoyed the Hitler Youth activities depended on the leadership of their group. As older members of the HJ moved on to military service, less talented leaders took over. The coming of war also changed the character of the HJ experience.

1   Why did young people join the Hitler Youth movements?

HJ Youth leaders undergoing medical inspections in September 1933

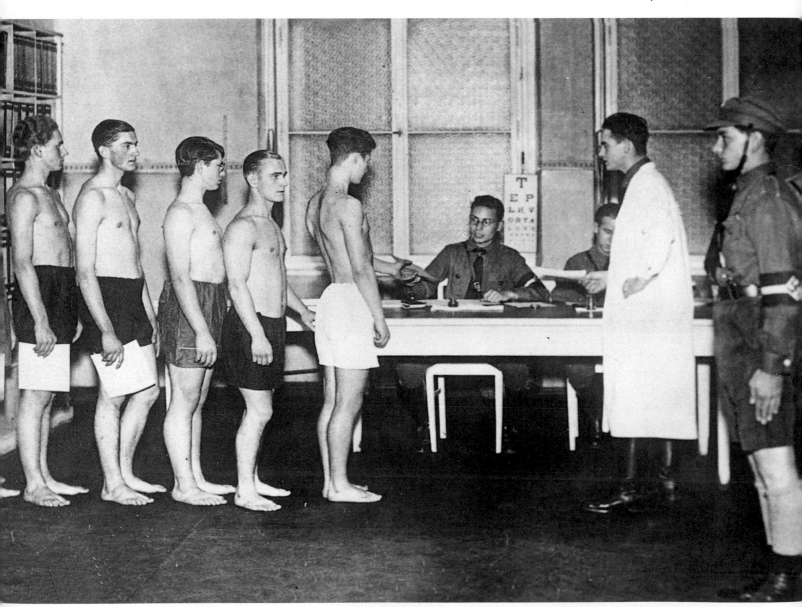

Did all young people welcome the Hitler Youth?

Detlev Peukert has studied the reactions of young people in Nazi Germany to the Hitler Youth movements. He believes that the experience of the Hitler Youth varies depending on when someone joined. Far from universal enthusiasm, some young people rejected the Hitler Youth.

Under the Nazis three separate age groups passed through adolescence (aged 14–18). Those from 1933–1936 had already had important experiences before the Nazis came to power. They had suffered the economic problems of the 1930s and, therefore, were receptive to the appeal of the rearmament programme. The youth of 1936–1939 had no such memories, they had gone through Nazi schools. For them there was no alternative to the Nazis. This group enjoyed the HJ as a rival to the traditional authorities of home and school. The age group whose adolescence fell between 1939–1945 experienced the empty aspects of the HJ full of drill and compulsion. This 'war generation' lost its leaders to the army and many of its club buildings to allied bombing. They found the HJ most irritating and increasingly repellent. For many young people the Nazi ideology seemed vague, as one said, 'No one in our class ever read *Mein Kampf*. On the whole we did not know much about Nazi ideas. We were politically programmed to obey and to stop thinking when the magic word "Fatherland" was uttered.'

For many young people the arrival of the Hitler Youth meant access to leisure activities for the first time. Girls had the chance to escape the female role-model centred on family and children. They could do things normally reserved for boys. The HJ concentrated in the late 1930s on bringing all young people in to their organisation. They carried out disciplinary and surveillance activities on their friends which caused great resentment. Many young people turned away from the HJ. They formed independent gangs and fought the Hitler Youth patrols. By the 1940s the Reich Youth leadership was worried that their influence was being undermined by these gangs. They could not blame this on 'Weimar', 'Communism' or the Churches. This opposing youth culture was the product of the Nazi system.

One notable group, the 'Edelweiss Pirates' (*Edelweissspiraten*), based around Essen, Düsseldorf and Cologne, went on weekend camping trips that involved 'bashing up' Hitler Youth patrols. The majority were from the working class who because of the war work were relatively well paid. To the Pirates, the HJ had few attractions.

A recruiting poster from 1944 announces the call up of all 17 year olds into the armed forces

Rebellious young people were punished. Twelve Edelweiss Pirates from Cologne were hanged in 1944 for sabotage, arms raids and anti-Nazi activities.

The title page of *Comradeship* an illegal underground youth magazine from 1938.

One of the Edelweiss Pirates from Düsseldorf, explained his group's slogan 'Eternal war on the Hitler Youth', 'It's the Hitler Youth's own fault, every order I was given contained a threat.' Their weekend trips allowed these young people some space and time away from adults and were made more attractive by the presence of girls. They adapted HJ songs with their own lyrics which reflected their anti-Nazi values. The Gestapo and Hitler Youth cracked down on these alternative youth groups. Warnings were given, members arrested (and released with their heads shaved), sent to labour camps or put on trial. Thousands were caught on a single day in Düsseldorf on 7 December 1942, and their ringleaders were hanged. Their activities ranged from deliberate non participation to open protest and resistance.

Another group were the middle class 'Swing Youth' (*Swingjugend*). It was inspired by English and American dance and jazz music. Banned from public gatherings by the Hitler Youth, clubs sprang up in Hamburg, Kiel, Berlin, Stuttgart, Frankfurt and Dresden. In Swing clubs young people danced the 'jitterbug', wore hair down to the collar and wore casual, fashionable English looking clothes. The Swing youth had a different identity to that of the HJ. They accepted Jews and admired the 'slovenly' culture of the wartime enemies, England and America. They upset the Nazi leaders. Himmler wanted to put the leaders of the Swing movement into concentration camps for at least three years of beatings, drill and forced labour.

The 'Pirate' and 'Swing' cultures show that even after years of power the Nazis still did not have a grip on German society. Indeed sections of it were slipping increasingly from its grasp.

Adapted from an article written by Detlev Peukert in 1985.

2 In what ways does Source B help us to assess the success of the Hitler Youth movements?

16 *T*he Nazis and education

> When an opponent declares, 'I will not join you', I calmly say, 'Your child belongs to us already. What are you? You will pass away and your descendants now stand in a new camp.'

Adolf Hitler, 1933.

B

Extracts from the Nazi newspaper, *Der Stürmer* being used in the classroom to teach children Nazi ideas about the Jews

The Nazis changed the education that young people received in schools. They used the schools as well as the Nazi Youth movements, to produce good young Nazis. The Nazis made changes that affected the teachers, the subjects taught, and the schools themselves. The teachers were persuaded by a mixture of propaganda and threat into joining the National Socialist Teachers' League (NSLB – *Nationalsozialistische Lehrerbund*). In January 1933 it had 6,000 members but by 1937 this had grown to 320,000 or 97% of the teaching profession. Teachers who wanted jobs or promotion had to be given a reference that they were good Nazis. The NSLB provided these references. That alone does not explain the popularity of the NSLB. There were many teachers in the Nazi Party. By 1934 nearly 25% of all teachers were Nazi Party members, whereas the total was only 10% for the population as a whole as late as 1939. The teachers, as civil servants had been particularly hit by the cuts in wages introduced during the economic crisis of 1929–1933 (see page 24). They turned to the Nazis in the hope that their pay, status and conditions would be improved.

They were soon disappointed in their hopes. Hitler and leading Nazis in their speeches showed that they had little respect for teachers, often open derision. Teachers saw no improvements in their pay, training and status. Their work was increasingly interfered with by the Hitler Youth. The teachers resented the crude Nazi propaganda produced for them and their students. Teachers became some of the Germans most disillusioned with the Nazis.

On 1 May 1934, Bernhard Rust was appointed to the new post of Reich Minister for Science and Education. He set up the first National Political Educational Institutions (*Napolas*) on Hitler's birthday, 20 April 1933. They were designed to provide the Nazi leaders of the future. These 23 elite schools were run by the SS after 1936. However, Schirach and the HJ (see page 71) were not content to leave the education of the next generation of Nazi leaders to Bernhard Rust, much to his annoyance. But Rust was not powerful enough to resist. In 1937 the Hitler Youth set up ten of their own elite, 'Adolf Hitler Schools' and for further training, students went on to one of three Nazi Colleges (*Ordensburgen*).

Bernard Rust, Reich Minister for Science and Education speaks in 1938, at a *Napola*, an elite SS school

of Physical Education. Those with physical handicaps were refused a secondary education. German language and literature work was carefully chosen to the show examples of German military success, of sacrifice for the Fatherland and the long traditions of the German people. Biology was an important subject because it was used to teach children about Nazi ideas on race. The Nazis made sure their ideas about inferior races were taught. Lessons explained the importance of making a racially sound marriage and the need to have children. They emphasised the natural law of selection. Lastly History was given a special place in the curriculum because through History children learnt about the greatness of the German nation.

The Nazis took control of the school curriculum in all German schools. They picked out the subjects which would help them to get Nazi ideas (see page 29) across to young people. German, History, Biology, and Physical Education were the most important school subjects for the Nazis. Physical Education such as gymnastics, athletics, and walking was essential for girls who would become the future mothers of the German nation. Boys would need to be fit and able to withstand physical hardship if they were to join the army to defend and expand the German Reich. They had to do at least five hours a week

D

A Russian soldier tried to get in his way, but Otto's bayonet slid gratingly between his ribs, so that he collapsed groaning. There it lay before him, simple and distinguished, his dream's desire, the Iron Cross.

Extract from a reading book for 14 year-olds, *The Battle of Tannenberg.*

A Nazi History lesson

A page from a Nazi school book for young children

Girls' School timetable

Periods	Monday	Tuesday	Wednesday	Thursday	Friday	Saturday
8.00–8.45	German	German	German	German	German	German
8.50–9.35	Geography	History	Singing	Geography	History	Singing
9.40–10.25	Race studies	Race studies	Race studies	Race studies	Race studies	Race studies
10.25–11.00	Break with Sports and special announcements					
11.00–12.05	Domestic Science with Mathematics					
12.10–12.55	Eugenics (the science of breeding) or Health Biology					
2.00–6.00	Sport					

I attended a class reunion in 1984, and this one woman said to me, 'You do know you were always an outsider? We could never stand you.' 'Why?' I asked. 'Because you were not athletic,' she replied. I was not unathletic but I did not like to take part in those big sports things. The woman went on, 'and because you were politically unreliable. Did you know I wanted to report you? Once you brought a sort of suitcase record player to school and played *The Threepenny Opera* during break to show us that this Jewish music is really very nice.' 'Why didn't you report me?' I asked. 'I talked about it with my parents and they said don't do it. You don't know who her parents are and what type of connections they have.'

Karma Raubut is reminded of her time in secondary school in 1942.

Führer, my Führer, sent to me by God,

Protect and preserve me all my life

You have rescued Germany
   in its hour of need

I thank you for my daily bread

Stay with me, never leave me,

Führer, My Führer, my faith and my light.

Children's Grace said before meals, 1936

1   By what methods did the Nazis try to change the education provided by German schools?

2   'A healthy man filled with decisiveness and strength of will is more valuable for the nation than an intelligent weakling' Adolf Hitler, *Mein Kampf.*

   How would schools under the Nazis have produced the sort of Germans Hitler wanted? Use all the sources and the information in the chapter to help you to explain your answer.

Teenage girls salute the flag at the start of school, 1935

17 *W*omen in the Nazi state

A Nazi poster from 1937 showing their support for family life. 'The Nazi party protects the national community (Volksgemeinschaft)'.

> The mission of women is to be beautiful and to bring children into the world. The female bird pretties herself for her mate and hatches eggs for him. In exchange, the male takes care of gathering the food and stands guard and wards off the enemy.

Josef Goebbels describes a woman's role in 1929.

Officially, the Nazis saw the part that women had to play in society as different but equally important to the role of men. According to the Nazis, nature had fitted women to that different role. A Nazi slogan summed it up when calling for women to be devoted to *Kinder, Küche und Kirche* (Children, Kitchen and Church). The Nazi leaders may have spoken of equality for women but they did not receive it inside the Nazi Party itself. The Party was dominated by men. There was not a single female Nazi member of the Reichstag and a Party rule of 1921 banned them from senior positions in the Nazi leadership. There were Nazi organisations for women like the NSF (*National Sozialistische Frauenschaft* – National Socialist Womanhood) and the DFW

 An SPD poster questions what women's lives will be like in the Third Reich, December 1930

(*Deutsches Frauenwerk* – German Women's Enterprise). They pumped out a propaganda message that the woman's place was in the home and organised courses on motherhood and home economics. The Nazis discouraged women from wearing modern fashions and makeup. In 1935 a Bavarian hotel banned, 'women with red nails and long trousers'; in Erfurt police stopped women smoking cigarettes in public.

The Nazis produced propaganda that praised women who stayed at home and had babies. They glorified the mother image, pregnant women were often described as 'bearing a child for the Führer'. On 12 August, the birthday of Hitler's own mother, they were awarded medals. 'The Mother Cross' (bronze, silver and gold), went to women who had more than four, six or eight children. After 1933 the Nazis made abortion illegal, restricted the availability of contraceptive advice and facilities, and greatly improved maternity benefits and family allowances. Women who were infertile could be divorced with ease. The Nazis were not just concerned with numbers, they wanted to improve the German race. This meant preventing some people from having children and encouraging others to have more. Their racial and eugenic policies allowed for the sterilisation of those people who had hereditary diseases, mental illness, or showed anti-social behaviour like alcoholism. By 1939 375,000 Germans had been forcibly sterilised. After 1935 Jewish women could not marry Aryan men. The other side of this eugenic policy was found in the SS-run *Lebensborn* (Spring of life) organisation which operated maternity homes to look after the orphaned or illegitimate children of racially sound Germans.

As well as trying to raise the birth-rate by encouraging women to have babies, the Nazis wanted women to give up paid work and return to the home. Between 1933 and 1936 married women were banned from the top professional jobs as doctors, lawyers and senior civil servants. From June 1933 interest free loans of 600 Reichmarks (about 4 months average industrial wage) were available to young women who left their jobs to get married. The labour exchanges and employers were asked to give first choice of jobs to men. However, this policy came under pressure in 1937 when Germany began to rearm.

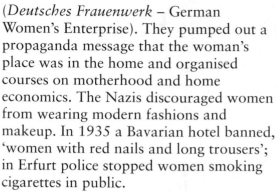

A poster advertising a Nazi approved film, 'Motherly love' which idealised the mother's role

1 How did the Nazis try to raise Germany's birth rate?
2 The following sources show different attitudes to women in the Third Reich. Why do you think this is so?

What explains Nazi attitudes to women?

Whatever the Nazis said in public, in their private thinking they believed women were by nature inferior to men. Hitler wanted to increase Germany's power and build an empire. The size of a country's population was a sign of its strength. Hitler had plans for expanding the borders of Germany. For this he needed a large and powerful army which in turn, required manpower. Unfortunately for Hitler, the German population had not been growing as fast as it had before. In 1901, 2,032,313 babies had been born, in 1932 this figure had fallen to 971,174. The growth of the German population was slowing down. Hitler's demands for *lebensraum* (living space) seemed weaker if the numbers of Germans was levelling out. This fact forced the Nazis to try to reverse the trend and get German women to have more babies. So women were encouraged to give up work and concentrate on the home.

The Nazis had another incentive to get women to give up work. They had been elected partly because they promised to provide more jobs. Every job left by a

woman returning to the home, was available for a man. However here again Hitler was fighting a powerful trend as more women had gone out to work during the First World War. They enjoyed the work and the income, despite earning about 60% of the male wage for the same job. When the war ended they stayed in work during the difficult, inflationary times of the 1920s. More work after the war favoured unskilled and cheaper women than men.

In their efforts the Nazis enjoyed some success. The numbers of working women only rose from 4.8 million in 1932 to 5.9 million in 1937, but because more men than women were taking jobs, this was really a fall from 37% to 31% of the total work force. But women were really too useful to the German economy to remove them completely from the work force. As the Nazis geared Germany up for war, women provided cheap and reliable labour. The Nazis relaxed the restrictions on women working from 1938. The Nazis were caught in the contradictions of their position.

C

If the man's world is the state, then the woman's world is her husband, her family, her children and her home. It is not correct for women to interfere in the world of man. The National Socialist Women's Movement has one single point – the child.

Adolf Hitler speaking to the National Socialist Women's Movement in September 1934.

The Nazi ideal of family life is captured in this propaganda photograph of an SS officer, his wife and children

B A propaganda poster from 1944 encouraging women to do all they can to support the war effort

D

E

Today man is educated not for, but against, marriage. We see our daughters growing up in stupid aimlessness living only in the vague hope of getting a man and having children. A son, even the youngest, laughs in his mother's face. He regards her as his servant and women in general as merely willing tools of his aims.

A letter to Hitler from several women, published in a Leipzig newspaper in 1934.

F

52 year old Aryan doctor. Fought in First World War. Wishes to settle down. Wants male children through marriage to a young, healthy, Aryan virgin. She should be undemanding, thrifty, used to heavy work, broad hipped, with flat heels and no earrings.

Advertisement for a wife.

G A German cartoon from the 1930s with the caption 'Introducing Frau Mueller who up to now has brought 12 children into the world.'

H

The SS guard, a Frau Lehmann, was in a rage, thrashing women prisoners with a club, hitting randomly. She pounded a group trying to hide behind the furniture. The SS women could really beat a prisoner. She didn't let anyone escape. We stood at the door watching and she turned to us and menacingly said, 'You all want to leave, don't you? It's time for me to go too. I have to feed my baby'. When she had gone I said to the girls, 'She must have sour milk in her breasts that one.' That was a *woman*. They were *beasts*.

Frau Lotte Müller, arrested as a Communist, describes a beating in the women's concentration camp of Ravensbrück, outside Berlin in 1942.

18 The economy under the Nazis

For Hitler the German economy was a way of getting what he wanted politically and militarily. Politically he wanted jobs. Hitler had promised to tackle unemployment in Germany. He wanted to keep his word and with it his popularity. Militarily Hitler wanted to expand Germany's borders, gaining land and resources. If he succeeded, Hitler would be fulfilling another promise, to make Germany great again. The economy had to provide the weapons to accomplish this and be organised so that it could carry out a long war – a 'defence economy' (*Wehrwirtschaft*). Hitler learned the lessons of 1918; a war on two fronts and the Allied blockade had led to defeat. With this in mind, Hitler wanted Germany to be self-sufficient in important raw materials and foods, yet provide the consumer goods Germans wanted.

Although Brüning negotiated the original reparations down to a token amount prior to the Lausanne conference in June 1932, Germany still owed large amounts borrowed to pay reparations under the Dawes and Young Plans. Germany was also importing raw materials for its work creation schemes and the wages paid to the workers were often spent on foreign made goods. Therefore, Germany was still buying more than it was making and selling abroad. Germany had not devalued the mark. This made German products more expensive than similar things from other countries, so German exports suffered.

The man Hitler chose to solve these problems was not a Nazi but the respected head of the Reichsbank, Hjalmar Schacht. From 3 July 1934, he was given wide powers as Economics Minister and brought in the 'New Plan'. The aim of the Plan was to provide Germany with the raw materials it needed for rearmament and public works without spending the little foreign money it had. The Plan put strict controls on imports that favoured raw materials and penalised consumer goods. Through the Plan Schacht made special arrangements to pay for raw materials from South America and South-east Europe with German-made goods. The 'New Plan' was successful. In 1935 Germany had a small trade surplus, unemployment was still falling and production had increased by nearly 50% since 1933.

However Schacht's clever financial schemes could not disguise the fact that Germany was still buying more than it was making and selling abroad. The drive for rearmament was the culprit. Schacht knew it and he asked for the pace to be slackened. This was something that Hitler and the powerful industrialists who profited from rearmament, would not do.

So in 1936 Hitler replaced Schacht with Goering. He brought in 'The Four Year Plan' which aimed to increase food production and achieve self-sufficiency in certain raw materials like oil, rubber, and metals. This would be done even if it meant making do with synthetic or *ersatz* substitutes. The success of the Plan was mixed. The planned production of aluminium, steel and explosives was nearly achieved but Goering failed to supply enough oil.

The results of these efforts have led historians to interesting conclusions. There is no mistaking where Hitler's plans were leading. However, when war broke out in 1939, the German economy was not ready for it. Germany had the resources only for short wars of the *Blitzkrieg* type. Hitler's plans for a world war would have been complete by 1943. The failure to take Moscow in 1941 was a turning point which came too soon for the German economy to cope.

'Hooray the butter is finished !' Goering said in his Hamburg speech, 'Ore has always made an empire strong, butter and lard have only made its people fat'.

Hurrah, die Butter ist alle!
Goering in seiner Hamburger Rede: „Erz hat stets ein Reich stark gemacht Butter und Schmalz haben höchstens ein Volk fett gemacht'

1 How is this 1935 picture by John Heartfield critical of the Nazis ?

Percentage of wealth (GNP) spent on military power			
	Germany	United Kingdom	United States
1932	1	1	1
1933	3	3	1
1934	6	3	1
1935	8	2	1
1936	13	2	1
1937	13	1	1
1938	17	8	1
1939	23	22	1
1940	38	53	2
1941	47	60	11
1942	55	64	31
1943	61	63	42
1944		62	42
1945		53	36

Were Germans better off under the Nazis?

Under the Nazis industrial workers enjoyed regular work and controlled shop prices. But their pay was also controlled and they had no trade unions to bargain for better conditions or higher wages. The average industrial worker's pay stayed the same from 1929 to 1938, however the average working week lengthened from 43 hours in 1933 to 47 hours in 1939. Average figures always disguise specific changes. Workers in the armament industries did improve their pay whereas those producing consumer goods earned less.

On 6 May 1933 the Nazis replaced the unions with DAF (*Deutsche Arbeitsfront* – German Labour Front) led by Dr Robert Ley. Membership was virtually compulsory for workers. In practice DAF was different from a union. It carried a massive responsibility for the operation of the workplace. At times taking the side of the employers, on other occasions supporting the workers but always looking to boost productivity for rearmament. To do this DAF stressed loyalty to the Nazi regime and tried to get the workers to see

German workers enjoying deck games on a 'Strength through Joy' (KDF) cruise holiday in 1935

themselves as an industrial community of workers and employers acting together. They should be motivated by a common spirit rather than by wages or profit. DAF ran two schemes to make this real to workers and to compensate for relatively static wages. The first was 'Beauty of Labour' (*Schönheit der Arbeit*), designed to improve working conditions in factories with slogans like 'Good lighting – good work' and 'Clean people in a clean plant'. This propaganda drive did not impress the workers as much as the second DAF initiative, 'Strength through Joy' (*Kraft durch Freude*). This programme appealed to the workers as consumers and offered incentives to work hard. In the absence of real pay rises for most workers it was well received. Free holidays, trips to concerts, and sporting events proved very popular.

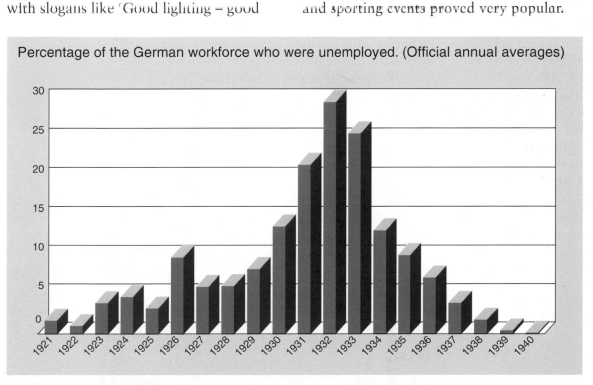

Percentage of the German workforce who were unemployed. (Official annual averages)

Reducing unemployment was one of Hitler's highest priorities. The *Law to Reduce Unemployment* passed on 1 June 1933 gave money to finance building projects throughout Germany and it insisted that the work be done manually wherever possible. On 27 June 1933 a law was passed to build the network of autobahns. In 1934 the push to rearm Germany began in earnest employers were encouraged to take on more workers and the country's unemployment began to fall dramatically. Under the Weimar Republic a Labour Service (*Arbietdienst*) had been created to absorb the unemployed workers. It fitted the Nazis' plans well and provided cheap labour. The *Reich Labour Law* of 26 June 1935 made labour service compulsory. In September 1935, Hitler made all young men between 18 and 25 do six months *Arbietdienst*. It was a chance for the Nazis to indoctrinate young people, keep them fit and further reduce unemployment. Many young people found the discipline of the service tough and the type of work dull and unpleasant. Unemployment figures also fell because the Jews were not counted, women were encouraged to leave full-time jobs, and the army was growing in size.

Many small farmers had supported the Nazis who promised to improve their lives. They also spoke highly of them as the reservoir of racially pure German people. They flattered them in propaganda with ideas like 'Blood and Soil' (*Blut und Boden*) which idealised the country life. Hitler needed the farmers to give Germany the self-sufficiency in food (*Nahrungsfreiheit*) that would make possible the expansion of the Reich. The Reich Food Estate (*Reichsnährstand*) under Richard Darré supervised agricultural production. The Nazis wanted stable prices and wages to avoid inflation and allow for rearmament. Darré kept food prices below their 1928–29 levels and set quotas for the food each farm should produce. This angered peasant farmers. On 29 September 1933 Darré passed the *Reich Entailed Farm Law* to protect 'the blood spring of the German nation'. It gave security to the peasant owners of average sized farms (7.5 to 125 hectares) who could not be thrown out for debts, but the law stopped them dividing up the farm between their heirs. The *Entailed Farm Law* was much resented by the farmers because it became more difficult to borrow money and more of their children moved to towns to seek industrial jobs and higher wages. Although the Nazis increased production of most foodstuffs, they failed miserably to increase the amount of fats being produced. Further progress for farmers was hampered because of the shortage of labour and the lack of money to buy machinery. Many of the older peasant farmers were disappointed. They could remember getting better prices for produce before the Nazis came to power. They were more concerned about the treatment of the Church than the threat of Communism. Younger farmers were more committed to the Nazis.

The middle class did not prosper under the Nazis. The small businesses upon which they were dependent were squeezed out by the big businesses. It was big businesses that did well because they could help with rearmament and benefited most from the reduced power of the trade unions. Under the Four Year Plan the number of self employed workers declined from 1.65 million to 1.5 million. The value of German companies' shares rose from 41 points in 1932 to 106 points in 1940.

2   Why is it difficult to decide if the Germans were better off under the Nazis?

19 *Resistance and opposition to Hitler*

It is time something must be done. Whoever acts will probably go down in German history as a traitor. Yet if he fails to act, he will be a traitor to his own conscience.

Colonel Claus von Stauffenberg, July 1944.

Opposition to Hitler and the Nazis existed in the 1920s and early 1930s from the established left-wing political parties – the Communists and the Social Democrats. In 1933 they had been banned. Both parties set up secret 'underground' organisations. The Communists were Hitler's declared enemies and had links with the Soviet Union. They tried to collect information that would help the Soviet Union through spy rings, the last of which was the *Rote Kapelle* (Red Orchestra) which was smashed by the Gestapo in August 1943. The Social Democrats (SPD) gathered information about the Nazis and, like the Communists, tried to stimulate resistance amongst factory workers through propaganda leaflets, illegal newspapers, and political discussions. Neither group co-operated with the other nor achieved any serious resistance. The Nazi police state was very effective at stifling critical voices and stamping out any threat.

As the true nature of the Nazi regime revealed itself, more people in the Church made efforts to resist it (see page 61). A Protestant minister and member of Niemöller's Confessing Church, Dietrich Bonhoeffer, made contact with the army officers opposed to Hitler. Bonhoeffer also sought Allied help. He was arrested in 1943 and executed in 1945. The Catholic Archbishop of Münster, Graf Clemens von Galen, spoke out bravely and successfully against the Nazis' euthanasia programme in 1941. Recognising his popularity the Nazis abandoned their programme.

With the retreat of the German armies in Russia in 1942, students at Munich University began producing anti-Nazi leaflets. The ringleaders of the White Rose Group, as it became known, were Hans and Sophie Scholl, along with Christoph Probst, Alex Schmorell, Willi Graf, and Professor Kurt Huber. It has been suggested

Hans and Sophie Scholl and Christoph Probst were the leaders of the White Rose Group, seen here in the summer of 1942

that they were inspired by Galen's protest. However it seems more likely that they were upset by the apathy of the people in the face of the crimes of the Nazis. As medical students, Hans Scholl, Graf, and Schmorell had served as orderlies on the Russian Front. They were well aware of the atrocities that took place there. After the Scholls distributed their final leaflets on 18 February 1943, they were denounced to the Gestapo. Condemned to death by a hastily summoned People's Court (Volksgerichtshof), the Scholls, Schmorell, Graf, Probst, and Huber were all sentenced to death and executed by guillotine on 22 February.

In the 1940s there was resistance from Germans much closer to the centre of government. They were disturbed by the brutality of the Nazis and alarmed by Hitler's plans for war. Meeting at Kreisau, the home of Helmuth von Moltke, the 'Kreisau Circle' were influential Germans who talked of ridding Germany of Hitler and the Nazis but they did nothing. A meeting planned between one of the them, Father Alfred Delp, and Professor Huber of the 'White Rose' did not take place because the Gestapo arrested Delp. The 'Kreisau Circle' were arrested and executed in 1944–5.

A more substantial opposition group formed around the former army leader, General Ludwig Beck who had resigned over Hitler's invasion of Austria in 1938, and Karl Goerdeler, a Nazi official replaced in 1936. From the time Hitler seemed to be moving towards war, many more highly placed Germans saw disaster ahead for Germany. They looked for help from those countries outside Germany who would also suffer if Hitler began another war. Britain was sceptical about the sincerity and effectiveness of the opposition. Hitler was after all the legitimate government in Germany. Even Hitler's removal would not guarantee that the Nazis would be replaced. The British believed that Hitler would be satisfied if his territorial demands were met. Britain kept the contacts with opposition groups alive but at arms length. Contacts were made between the Kreisau Circle and the Beck-Goerdeler group but they could not agree. The Beck-Goerdeler was more right-wing and nationalist than the Kreisau Circle, and more willing to take decisive, violent action to remove Hitler. They had the support of others in the army and could get close to the Führer. Having failed to prevent war, when it came, they tried to end it quickly. By 1942 they agreed that Hitler would have to be killed. There were two small scale attempts in March and November 1943 and then the 'July Plot' in 1944.

On 20 July 1944 they planned and carried out an attempt to blow up Hitler at his 'wolf's lair' headquarters in East Prussia. Colonel Claus von Stauffenberg arrived with a bomb in his briefcase. He placed it under the table, two metres away from Hitler. He set the fuse and left the room to make 'an urgent phone call'. At 12.42 an explosion shattered the room.

Adolf Hitler greets General Fromm at the 'Wolf's lair' headquarters in East Prussia on 15 July 1944. On the far left is Colonel Claus von Stauffenberg who, five days later, planted the bomb that nearly killed Hitler.

Hitler cut, covered with dust and deafened, survived. Someone had moved the briefcase to the other side of a table leg and the heavy table top had saved him. Stauffenberg, thinking Hitler was dead, was already on his way to Berlin. Stauffenberg was arrested and shot by the Gestapo. Hitler took a savage revenge on all those involved in the 'July Plot'. The official list of those executed runs to 5,746 and included 19 generals, 26 colonels, 7 diplomats, 2 ambassadors, 1 minister, and the Chief of the Criminal Police. The failure of the plot brought the German army under the tight control of the SS.

 One of Hitler's staff shows the trousers that the Führer wore on 20 July 1944, the day Stauffenberg's bomb exploded

1   In this chapter and chapters 7, 10–13 and 15 you will find information about the resistance to Hitler and the Nazis. Describe what individuals and groups did to oppose the Nazis.
2   Why was so little achieved by the resistance to Hitler?

 Plötzensee prison where the Stauffenberg plotters were hanged slowly by piano wire from meat hooks or beheaded. Over 200 people were executed here. Hitler took great pleasure in looking at the photographs of their last moments.

1 The regime still controls the instruments of power and propaganda. Hundreds of thousands of supporters depend for their jobs
5 and prosperity on the continuation of the regime. Those at the top have no scruples and will not shrink from the greatest crimes. The weakness of the
10 opposition is the strength of the regime. The middle class and peasants criticise mainly from self-interest, they are not prepared to fight because they do not know what they
15 should be fighting for. Fear of Communism, of chaos which would follow the fall of Hitler is still the negative foundation of Nazi power. The left is split into Communists and
20 Socialists and many other factions. The Churches attitude is not uniform and is directed to improving their position *within* the regime. (**1934**)

The Nazis have persuaded the
25 masses to leave politics to the men at the top. They will never succeed in turning everyone into committed Nazis. People turn inwardly away from Nazism. (**Westphalia, 1936**)

30 The majority of the population looking at Communism, say 'Well, I'd rather have Hitler' (**1936**).

Everyone tries to get out of attending big events such as 1 May.
35 There is no longer any point in attending meetings. Pub landlords complain most bitterly at the fall off in trade. People say 'If one cannot say what one thinks in public it is better to
40 stay at home. One does not let rip for fear of ending up in Dachau'. (**Württemberg, 1937**)

It seems to us that the indifference which has gripped the population has
45 become the second pillar supporting the system. People simply want to get by and know nothing about what is going on around them. That suits the Nazis fine. Only shortages of food
50 cause slight grumblings but there is no enthusiasm, only from school children and those yet to do their military service. (**Saxony, 1938**)

The whole nation is convinced Hitler
55 is a great politician. This is solely due to his foreign policy successes. (**Danzig, 1939**)

Many members of the SPD fled Germany in 1933. Their contacts within the country sent reports to their base in Prague until 1938 when they moved to Paris and then London (1941). These extracts are from reports made during Nazi rule.

3 'People turn inwardly away from Nazism' (lines 28–29). People coped with Nazism by what was called 'inner emigration'. What does this mean?

4 How do these extracts help us to explain the lack of resistance to the Nazis?

5 How reliable are these reports of the German people's views under the Nazis?

20 *The Hitler myth*

Adolf Hitler (1889–1945) seen here in 1931. On the right is Rudolf Hess (1894–1987), Deputy Leader of the Nazi Party.

Look now at the face of Germany, we see that a master builder is behind it – the master builder that God has given us. Looking at the events of the last two thousand years, we can see that the final shape has now been found. To be allowed to serve Adolf Hitler is a gift of Heaven. In Hitler the longing of millions upon millions of our German people has become a reality.

From a Munich newspaper, 21 April 1933.

Hitler enjoyed remarkable popularity because of the myth he created about his leadership. It became a cult nourished by propaganda. Hitler was portrayed as heroic, dynamic and charismatic. A leader who was in contrast to the other drab Weimar politicians. He offered change. His ideas of German nationalism and opposition to Socialism, Weimar and Versailles had wide appeal. The cult had for some Germans a religious character with Hitler as Germany's saviour. There were several elements to the Hitler myth.

- Hitler stood for the enforcement of law and order, he voiced the people's feelings and sense of justice. He cleared away the enemies of the German nation.
- Hitler represented the national interest. He was above party or selfish motives. Excesses, greed, errors were the work of other Party officials. Hitler was unaware of them.
- Hitler had made life better for the people. They enjoyed prosperity and work because of him.
- Hitler was a moderate who was against the extreme Nazis. Hitler was a sincere and God fearing man.
- Hitler was uncompromising, a fanatic committed to ruthless action against the enemies of the people. But he only agreed to 'lawful' and 'rational' action not crude violence or public brutality.
- Hitler was a man of peace, a defender of Germany's rights, a righter of wrongs, a statesman and rebuilder of national pride.
- Hitler was a brilliant military strategist.

1   What evidence can you find from a study of Nazi Germany that challenges or supports the elements of the Hitler myth?
2   Why do you think Source B is critical of Hitler?

▲ 200,000 Germans came to listen to Chancellor Hitler's May Day speech in Berlin on 1 May 1934

Judging Hitler and the Germans. This cartoon appeared in *The Sunday Dispatch* in 1943. Would you agree with the cartoonist's view of the Germans?

RELIGIOUS FREEDOM suppressed — ACADEMIC FREEDOM suppressed — LABOR UNIONS FRATERNAL ORGANISATIONS OPPOSITION PARTIES suppressed — WOMENS INDEPENDENCE suppressed — FREEDOM of the PRESS suppressed — JUDICIAL INTEGRITY suppressed

"In these three years I have restored honor and freedom to the German people!"

HITLER IS BAD — WELL, THERE'S NO ARGUMENT ABOUT THAT.....

GÖRING — HE'S HOPELESS!..

GOEBBELS — BECAUSE HE'S THE BIGGEST LIAR EVER...

RIBBENTROP — WHAT A CROOK!---

HIMMLER BECAUSE HE'S A MASS MURDERER...

THE REST OF THE GANG BECAUSE THEY ARE THE BIGGEST BUNCH OF CRIMINALS EVER TO GET TOGETHER.....

.... THEN THERE'S THE 17,265,823 VOTERS WHO PUT THE NAZIS INTO POWER IN 1933. AND THE 98.79 PER CENT OF THE GERMAN PEOPLE WHO VOTED TO KEEP THEM THERE IN 1936 ....

...AND DON'T FORGET THE REST OF THE 80 MILLIONS WHO ARE ALSO ENJOYING THE LOOT OF THE OCCUPIED COUNTRIES.......

BUT LET US BE FAIR — THERE ARE SOME GOOD GERMANS — AND THEIR NUMBERS ARE GROWING EVERY DAY.

What was Hitler's role?

An American magazine, *The Nation*, 5 February 1936, comments on Hitler's achievements. In a plebiscite on 29 March 1936, following the German reoccupation of the Rhineland, 98.8% of the votes cast supported the Government.

1 In Hitler's Reich there was no clear administrative structure or straightforward chain of command.
5 Obviously the Nazi Party was powerful and influenced ordinary Germans through organisations like the Hitler Youth, but the relationship between the Party and the State was
10 unclear. If Hitler wanted a particular task done he often created a special agency like the Four Year Plan Organisation. Was it that Hitler couldn't be bothered to make an efficient system of government or did
15 he prefer to have groups and individuals competing for power because it strengthened his own position as Führer? Because there
20 was no clear cut line of command it was difficult and dangerous to challenge Hitler. He could intervene at will, although he was lazy about administrative matters and left
25 subordinates like Himmler to develop their own mini-empires. Maybe through laziness or arrogance those beneath him had to compete for influence. Hitler was not interested in
30 genuine discussion. He held few cabinet meetings and votes were not taken. Hitler usually issued edicts. A minister who got his signature did not have to consult others. Hitler did not
35 allow his subordinates to know more than they needed. It was a personal system of power.

There has been much debate about Hitler's exact role in the Third Reich.
40 Did he use the 'divide and rule' method or was he the object of competing groups, institutions and individuals all trying to exploit his lack of interest in systematic government?
45 Hitler had no need of a 'divide and rule' policy, there was no one seriously trying to replace him but many tried to win him over to their point of view. It is possible to interpret
50 Hitler's role in various ways in different situations. Certainly he blocked attempts to streamline decision making probably out of distrust at any move to restrict his
55 own power. Yet certain individuals were allowed to build up their own power bases like Robert Ley and Martin Bormann. It seems that Hitler expected loyalty and if he got it he
60 turned a blind eye to some activities. Sometimes he intervened, usually he preferred to stay aloof. Whether deliberate or not this tactic had one great advantage. It put Hitler above
65 popular criticism. It would be wrong to describe Hitler as a weak dictator. Arbitrary and sometimes impulsive, when he *did* want his way, he got it. There are no major decisions in
70 foreign policy on which Hitler was blocked by subordinates and in domestic policy, he was never unhappy with the direction of events. It is misleading to talk about a
75 coherent social and economic policy but he could have intervened when ever he wished. Although Hitler might hesitate and agonise, he did act, so he cannot be accused of lacking
80 firmness of purpose.

Adapted from *Hitler: Germany's fate or Germany's misfortune* by John Laver, 1995.

3 Read Source C. What is its view of Hitler's style and role in government?
4 In what ways did Hitler's style of government reinforce the Hitler myth?
5 Consider the following aspects of the Third Reich

a The Economy
b Racial policy
c The Police state.
In what ways do Hitler's actions in these areas reflect his style of government and leadership?

Index